ASIAN POLITICAL, ECONOMIC AND SECURITY ISSUES

THAILAND

CONDITIONS, ISSUES AND U.S. RELATIONS

ASIAN POLITICAL, ECONOMIC AND SECURITY ISSUES

Additional books in this series can be found on Nova's website under the Series tab.

Additional E-books in this series can be found on Nova's website under the e-book tab.

ASIAN POLITICAL, ECONOMIC AND SECURITY ISSUES

THAILAND

CONDITIONS, ISSUES AND U.S. RELATIONS

KENNY N. CADE
EDITOR

New York

For permission to use material from this book please contact us:
Telephone 631-231-7269; Fax 631-231-8175
Web Site: http://www.novapublishers.com

Additional color graphics may be available in the e-book version of this book.

LIBRARY OF CONGRESS CATALOGING-IN-PUBLICATION DATA

ISBN: 978-1-63117-596-1

Published by Nova Science Publishers, Inc. † New York

CONTENTS

Preface		**vii**
Chapter 1	Thailand: Background and U.S. Relations *Emma Chanlett-Avery and Ben Dolven*	**1**
Chapter 2	Thailand 2012 Human Rights Report *U.S. Department of State; Bureau of Democracy, Human Rights and Labor*	**33**
Chapter 3	Thailand 2012 International Religious Freedom Report *U.S. Department of State; Bureau of Democracy, Human Rights and Labor*	**93**
Chapter 4	2013 Investment Climate Statement: Thailand *Bureau of Economic and Business Affairs*	**105**
Index		**141**

PREFACE

This book provides a background of Thailand and U.S. relations. It also discusses Thailand's 2012 international religious freedom report along with a 2013 investment climate statement.

Chapter 1 – U.S.-Thailand relations are of interest to Congress because of Thailand's status as a long-time military ally and a significant trade and economic partner. For many years, Thailand was also seen as a model of stable democracy in Southeast Asia, although this image, along with U.S. relations, have been complicated by deep political and economic instability in the wake of a September 2006 coup that displaced Prime Minister Thaksin Shinawatra, a popular but divisive figure who remains a flashpoint for many divisions within Thailand.

In recent years, Thai politics have been dominated by rivalries between populist forces led by Thaksin (now in exile) and his opponents, a mix of conservative royalists and military figures, and other Bangkok elites. Despite his exile, pro-Thaksin political parties have won the three nationwide elections since his ouster, and the current government is led by his younger sister, Yingluck Shinawatra. Mass movements both supporting and opposing Thaksin have staged vigorous demonstrations, including protests in 2010 that spilled over to riots in Bangkok and other cities, causing the worst street violence in Thailand in decades. Large-scale anti-Thaksin demonstrations in November and December 2013 forced Prime Minister Yingluck to dissolve Parliament and call for nationwide elections in February 2014.

Many analysts believe traditional Thai elites—particularly the military's top brass and many prominent royalist figures—remain deeply opposed to Thaksin and any indication that he might seek to return to a political role in Thailand. But Thaksin (and Yingluck) have considerable support in the country's poorer regions, stemming from programs Thaksin pursued during his rule from 2001-2006 to provide rural healthcare and other benefits, which have continued under Yingluck. Thaksin's ouster has brought out divisions that had been emerging for years between the growing middle-class and the poorer rural population. Risks are heightened by uncertainty about the health of Thailand's widely revered King Bhumiphol Adulyadej, who is 86 and has been hospitalized for much of the past four years.

Despite past differences on Burma policy and human rights issues, shared economic and security interests have long provided the basis for U.S.-Thai cooperation. Thailand contributed troops and support for U.S. military operations in both Afghanistan and Iraq and was designated as a major non-NATO ally in December 2003. Thailand's airfields and ports play a particularly important role in U.S. global military strategy, including having served as the primary hub of the relief effort following the 2004 Indian Ocean tsunami and the 2008 Cyclone Nargis in Burma. In 2012, Thailand was the 25th largest goods trading partner of the United States, with over $37 billion in two-way trade, and the United States is Thailand's largest export market.

Although the alliance itself does not appear to be fundamentally shaken by Thailand's political events of the past few years, Bangkok's reliability as a partner, and its ability to be a regional leader, are uncertain. Successive Thai governments have also been unable to stem violence by insurgents in the southern majority-Muslim provinces. Under the Obama Administration, the United States has prioritized engagement with Southeast Asia and a broader strategic rebalancing towards the Asia-Pacific, but many observers argue that broad new initiatives with Thailand have been notably lacking. With its favorable geographic location and broad-based economy, Thailand has traditionally been considered among the most likely countries to play a major leadership role in the region. But growing U.S. engagement with other allies and partners such as the Philippines and Singapore, and Thailand's domestic problems appear to have dimmed the prominence of the U.S.-Thai relationship in Southeast Asia. Thailand maintains close relations with China and is considered by some to be a key arena of competition between Beijing and Washington for influence.

Chapter 2 – Thailand is a constitutional monarchy with a revered king who has traditionally exerted strong influence. A coalition government led by Yingluck Shinawatra and her Puea Thai (For Thais) Party came to power in August 2011 following national elections in July for the National Assembly lower house that were generally viewed as free and fair. Security forces reported to civilian authorities.

The most persistent human rights problems included abuses by government security forces and local defense volunteers in the context of the continuing Muslim separatist insurgency in the South; the continued reported use at times of excessive force by security forces, including police killing, torturing, and otherwise abusing criminal suspects, detainees, and prisoners; and continued government limits on freedom of speech and press.

Other human rights problems included continued poor, overcrowded, and unsanitary prison and detention facilities; occasional arbitrary arrests and detention; government limits on freedom of assembly; insufficient protection for vulnerable populations, including refugees; violence and discrimination against women; sex tourism; sexual exploitation of children; trafficking in persons; discrimination against persons with disabilities, minorities, hill tribe members, and foreign migrant workers; child labor; and some limitations on worker rights.

Authorities occasionally dismissed, arrested, prosecuted, and convicted security force members who committed abusive behavior, but official impunity continued to be a serious problem, especially in provinces where the 2005 Emergency Decree, the 2008 Internal Security Act, and martial law remained invoked.

In the southernmost provinces, the great majority of victims of the violence associated with the separatist insurgency were civilians not taking an active part in hostilities.

Chapter 3 – The constitution and other laws and policies protect religious freedom and, in practice, the government generally respected religious freedom, although there were some reports of abuses and the government restricted the activity of certain groups. The trend in the government's respect for religious freedom did not change significantly during the year.

There were reports of societal abuses based on religious affiliation, belief or practice. In the southernmost border provinces, continued separatist violence contributed to tense relations between ethnic Thai Buddhist and ethnic Malay Muslim communities. While the conflict in the South primarily involves ethnicity and nationalism, the close affiliation between ethnic and religious identity caused it to take on religious overtones. As a result violence in the region undermined citizens' abilities to undertake the full range of their religious activities in a number of cases.

The U.S. government discussed religious freedom with the government, visited religious leaders, hosted interreligious events, and promoted educational exchanges with the United States that supported religious freedom and tolerance.

Chapter 4 – Despite internal political tensions and severe flooding in 2011, Thailand continues to maintain an open, market-oriented economy and encourages foreign direct investment as a means of promoting economic development, employment, and technology transfer. In recent decades, Thailand has been a major destination for foreign direct investment, and hundreds of U.S. companies have invested in Thailand successfully. Thailand continues to welcome investment from all countries and seeks to avoid dependence on any one country as a source of investment. Following the significant impact of flooding in late 2011, investors are seeking development and implementation of an improved government water management plan as a critical element to maintaining investor confidence.

With flooding affecting 60 of 77 provinces, especially manufacturers in key industrial estates in Bangkok and its five surrounding provinces, a sharp contraction of nearly 9 percent occurred in the fourth quarter, wiping out 3.2 percent (year-on-year) growth during the first three quarters to only a mere 0.1 percent for the 2011 full-year GDP. However, the Thai economy remains resilient in the face of the severe domestic floods and continuing global economic crises. After the flat growth in 2011, recovery from the floods was satisfyingly rapid during the first three quarters of 2012 (2.6 percent) due to robust domestic demand from reconstruction and the government's stimulus programs. With low base effect during the last quarter, the government anticipated the 2012 full-year growth at a rate of 5.5 percent. Concerns over fleeing foreign investors out of the country also proved largely unfounded.

In the wake of the 1997-98 Asian Financial Crisis, Thailand embarked on an International Monetary Fund (IMF)-sponsored economic reform program designed to foster a more competitive and transparent climate for foreign investors. Legislation in 1999 established a new bankruptcy court, reformed bankruptcy, and foreclosure procedures, and allowed creditors to pursue payment from loan guarantors. Other 1999 reforms include amendments to the Land Code, Condominium Act, and the Property Leasing Act, all of which liberalized restrictions on property ownership by non-Thais. The Foreign Business Act (FBA) of 1999 continues to govern most investment activity by non-Thai nationals. The FBA opened some additional business sectors to foreign investment; however, foreign investment in most service sectors is limited to 49 percent ownership. Other key laws governing foreign investment are Alien Employment Act B.E. 2521 (1978) and Investment Promotion Act B.E. 2520 (1977).

Foreign companies are free to open and maintain bank accounts in foreign currency. However, Thailand retains to some extent its investment control, as under certain circumstances, foreign investors that are previously granted national treatment are subject to some reservations, in particular the service sector. From January 2012, the lower corporate tax rate was reduced from 30 percent to 23 percent, and will be cut further to 20 percent from January 2013 onward. Benefits of the lower corporate tax rate, however, may be offset by an increase of daily minimum wage rate of around 40 percent in April 2012 and by another 22.4 percent to a uniform Thai Baht300 per day ($10) in January 2013 nationwide.

In: Thailand
Editor: Kenny N. Cade

ISBN: 978-1-63117-596-1

Chapter 1

THAILAND: BACKGROUND AND U.S. RELATIONS*

Emma Chanlett-Avery and Ben Dolven

SUMMARY

U.S.-Thailand relations are of interest to Congress because of Thailand's status as a long-time military ally and a significant trade and economic partner. For many years, Thailand was also seen as a model of stable democracy in Southeast Asia, although this image, along with U.S. relations, have been complicated by deep political and economic instability in the wake of a September 2006 coup that displaced Prime Minister Thaksin Shinawatra, a popular but divisive figure who remains a flashpoint for many divisions within Thailand.

In recent years, Thai politics have been dominated by rivalries between populist forces led by Thaksin (now in exile) and his opponents, a mix of conservative royalists and military figures, and other Bangkok elites. Despite his exile, pro-Thaksin political parties have won the three nationwide elections since his ouster, and the current government is led by his younger sister, Yingluck Shinawatra. Mass movements both supporting and opposing Thaksin have staged vigorous demonstrations, including protests in 2010 that spilled over to riots in Bangkok and other cities, causing the worst street violence in Thailand in decades. Large-

* This is an edited, reformatted and augmented version of a Congressional Research Service publication, CRS Report for Congress RL32593, from www.crs.gov, prepared for Members and Committees of Congress, dated December 20, 2013.

scale anti-Thaksin demonstrations in November and December 2013 forced Prime Minister Yingluck to dissolve Parliament and call for nationwide elections in February 2014.

Many analysts believe traditional Thai elites—particularly the military's top brass and many prominent royalist figures—remain deeply opposed to Thaksin and any indication that he might seek to return to a political role in Thailand. But Thaksin (and Yingluck) have considerable support in the country's poorer regions, stemming from programs Thaksin pursued during his rule from 2001-2006 to provide rural healthcare and other benefits, which have continued under Yingluck. Thaksin's ouster has brought out divisions that had been emerging for years between the growing middle-class and the poorer rural population. Risks are heightened by uncertainty about the health of Thailand's widely revered King Bhumiphol Adulyadej, who is 86 and has been hospitalized for much of the past four years.

Despite past differences on Burma policy and human rights issues, shared economic and security interests have long provided the basis for U.S.-Thai cooperation. Thailand contributed troops and support for U.S. military operations in both Afghanistan and Iraq and was designated as a major non-NATO ally in December 2003. Thailand's airfields and ports play a particularly important role in U.S. global military strategy, including having served as the primary hub of the relief effort following the 2004 Indian Ocean tsunami and the 2008 Cyclone Nargis in Burma. In 2012, Thailand was the 25th largest goods trading partner of the United States, with over $37 billion in two-way trade, and the United States is Thailand's largest export market.

Although the alliance itself does not appear to be fundamentally shaken by Thailand's political events of the past few years, Bangkok's reliability as a partner, and its ability to be a regional leader, are uncertain. Successive Thai governments have also been unable to stem violence by insurgents in the southern majority-Muslim provinces. Under the Obama Administration, the United States has prioritized engagement with Southeast Asia and a broader strategic rebalancing towards the Asia-Pacific, but many observers argue that broad new initiatives with Thailand have been notably lacking. With its favorable geographic location and broad-based economy, Thailand has traditionally been considered among the most likely countries to play a major leadership role in the region. But growing U.S. engagement with other allies and partners such as the Philippines and Singapore, and Thailand's domestic problems appear to have dimmed the prominence of the U.S.-Thai relationship in Southeast Asia. Thailand maintains close relations with China and is considered by some to be a key arena of competition between Beijing and Washington for influence.

INTRODUCTION

An American treaty ally since 1954, Thailand has long been praised as an economic and democratic success story. The U.S.-Thai relationship, solidified during the Cold War, has expanded on the basis of shared economic and security interests. Thailand is a large trade and investment partner for the United States, and U.S. access to Thai military facilities and sustained military-to-military cooperation make Thailand an important element of the U.S. strategic presence in the Asia-Pacific region.

The country's political stability and democratic development have been shaken, however, by extensive political turmoil in the wake of a September 2006 coup by the Thai military that deposed Prime Minister Thaksin Shinawatra, a populist tycoon whose political party had won two parliamentary elections. Thaksin's rise—and then his fall and its aftermath—exposed deep and lasting divisions within Thai society, largely between urban elites and politically isolated rural Thais, who Thaksin courted with populist economic programs. The coup also set off power struggles among established power centers, which spilled over into unprecedented street violence in 2010 and large demonstrations in late 2013 by protestors calling for the government to stop down and, in some form, an alteration of the country's political system.

Thailand's economy has continued to grow strongly through the turmoil, and it remains an economically vibrant middle-income nation and a strong security partner for the United States. The turmoil, though, has called into question its democratic development and its ability to take leadership on regional or global issues. Thaksin remains in exile, and would face a two-year prison sentence for corruption should he return to Thailand. His younger sister, Yingluck Shinawatra, heads Thailand's government and has called for nationwide Parliamentary elections on February 2, 2014.

The political turmoil has presented myriad challenges for the United States. In the aftermath of the 2006 coup, the United States strove to maintain the relationship while simultaneously imposing penalties for the interruption of democratic rule. Military aid, suspended after the coup, was reinstated after elections in December 2007, but as successive Thai governments struggled to hold on to power, new uncertainty about the durability of the alliance and Thailand's commitment to democratic rule emerged.[1]

A stable Thailand is strategically important to the United States, both because of its status as a U.S. treaty ally and as an anchor for mainland Southeast Asia. U.S. policymakers are faced with how to deal with an unraveling democracy and how to respond to profound concerns about the civilian-military balance in Thai society. Many analysts consider Thailand to be so preoccupied with political infighting that its regional influence has waned. At an operational level the alliance continues to function largely smoothly, but new strategic initiatives have languished. When the Obama Administration announced a series of moves in late 2011 to "rebalance" U.S. foreign policy priorities to the Asia-Pacific region, including considerable deepening of regional alliances, new moves in the U.S.-Thailand alliance were notably lacking. The country is not part of the Administration's signature economic initiative in the region, the Trans-Pacific Partnership (TPP) trade negotiations.

Two fundamental questions hang over Thailand's political landscape. One is the prospect of Thaksin's possible return. Thaksin has remained highly prominent and visible overseas—in April 2012, for instance, he demonstrated his continued support when he made a public appearance in neighboring Cambodia during the Thai New Year holiday, telling an estimated 50,000 Thai visitors that he would "soon" return home.[2] An amnesty bill that would have cleared his criminal charges and facilitated his return was the trigger for the large protests that began in October 2013. The other critical question surrounds Thailand's King, Bhumiphol Adulyadej, who is 86 and reportedly in poor health. The King is widely adored, and for most of the past six decades, the monarchy has been Thailand's most stable institution. As the question of monarchical succession nears, however, the potential for further instability emerging from that event has become a strong concern.

One of the primary motivations for maintaining strong relations with Bangkok is the ongoing competition with Beijing for influence in Southeast Asia. Thailand, long known for its ability to keep good relations with all parties, enjoys strong economic, political, and cultural ties with both China and the United States. A stronger, more outward-looking Thailand could also provide support for many of the Administration's "rebalancing" initiatives.

DEVELOPMENTS IN LATE 2013

Demonstrations of 2013, and Call for New Elections

The relative stability that had taken hold since Yingluck took office in 2011 fractured again in the fall of 2013. After the ruling party tried to pass a general amnesty bill in October 2013 that would have cleared Thaksin from his corruption conviction (as well as several opposition leaders from charges related to the 2010 protests), protests erupted anew in the streets of Bangkok. The demonstrators, reported to be up to 200,000 at their peak, occupied several government compounds and created gridlock in areas of the capital city. Protest leaders called for the end of the "Thaksin regime" and demanded that a "people's council" reporting to the King replace Parliament. Parties aligned with Thaksin have won each of the five general elections since 2001. In early December, Yingluck called for new elections, setting the date for February 2, 2014, but protesters refused to disperse. The palace endorsed the election date but the ailing King has not intervened in the latest political crisis.

The State Department issued a statement that "The United States strongly supports democratic institutions and the democratic process in Thailand," and called on the parties to "resolve political differences peacefully and democratically in a way that reflects the will of the Thai people and strengthens the rule of law."

CURRENT STATE OF U.S.-THAI RELATIONS

Throughout Thailand's prolonged period of political instability, the Bangkok-Washington relationship has remained stable, although not flourishing. U.S. officials have voiced their concerns with some of the government's policies, particularly the curtailment of Thai citizens' rights under the state of emergency decree (now lifted). Overall, the long-standing relationship appears to have weathered the crises thus far, and has remained engaged in high-level dialogues. President Obama visited Bangkok in November 2012 as part of his first overseas trip following his re-election.

However, the opportunity costs of Thailand's political turmoil may have been high, as the Obama Administration has announced a rebalancing of U.S. foreign policy priorities towards Asia without a major Thai component. Domestic problems in Thailand have consumed the government's energy and ability to play a strong leadership role in the region, and Washington has looked to other allies and partners like Australia, the Philippines, and Singapore, as well as new partnerships with countries like Indonesia and Vietnam.

U.S. military officials are keen to maintain strong links with the Thai military establishment, particularly given the strategic value of Thai facilities in possible regional contingencies. Some regional analysts insist that Thailand, while imperfect, is an important democratic ally and crucial to indicate U.S. commitment to the region. However, criticism has emerged that U.S. efforts to instill core concepts like civilian control of the military appear to have had little effect given the experience of the past few years. Although use of Thai airfields has been crucial in U.S military operations and relief efforts, some observers doubt that Thailand would allow the United States to use the facilities in some potential conflicts.

Yet bilateral engagement has continued, particularly in the traditional areas of security cooperation. Thailand continues to host the annual large-scale multinational Cobra Gold military exercises and hosted a capacity-building exercise for the U.S.-led Proliferation Security Initiative, a multinational effort that aims to interdict vessels carrying weapons or illicit materials.

THAILAND POLITICS AND GOVERNMENT

Background

The Kingdom of Thailand, a constitutional monarchy with a parliamentary form of government, is marked by an important historical dissimilarity from its regional neighbors. Although occupied by Japan during World War II, Thailand was the only country in Southeast Asia that was not colonized by Europeans, and it also avoided the wave of communist revolutions that took control of the neighboring governments of Cambodia, Laos, and Vietnam in the 1960s and 1970s. Thailand followed a troubled path to democracy, enduring a series of mostly bloodless coups and multiple changes of government in its modern history. Although Thailand became a constitutional monarchy in 1932, it was ruled primarily by military dictatorships until the early 1990s. A military and bureaucratic elite controlled Thai politics during this period, denying room for civilian democratic institutions to develop. Brief periods of democracy in the 1970s and 1980s ended with reassertions of military rule. After Thai soldiers killed at least 50 people in demonstrations demanding an end to military dominance of the government, international and domestic pressure led to new elections in 1992. The 2006 coup was the first in 15 years.

Thailand's government is composed of the executive branch (prime minister as head of government and the king as chief of state), a bicameral National Assembly, and a judicial branch of three court systems. In the years immediately preceding Thaksin's election in 2001, the Democrat Party dominated Thai politics by instituting a series of reforms that enhanced transparency, decentralized power from the urban centers, tackled corruption, and introduced a broad range of constitutional rights.

Social Divisions and the Thai Political Landscape

The recent political turmoil in Thailand underscores a growing divide between the rural, mostly poor population and the urban middle class, largely based in Bangkok. By stoking Thai nationalism and providing inexpensive health care and other support to rural communities, Thaksin galvanized a populist movement in Thailand, with the support leading to emphatic electoral victories for his Thai Rak Thai Party, then the successor People's Power Party (PPP), and now the Puea Thai Party. This success threatened the traditional model of governance, which combines a powerful military backed by the royal family, an elite corps of bureaucrats, and a relatively weak executive government. Thaksin's rise and fall—and the role he continues to play in Thai politics—did much to expose and exacerbate the country's regional and class-based rifts.

These divisions have been emerging for years, but many hoped that the reckoning could unfold without bloodshed. The confrontation is no longer as simple as a conflict between mostly poor, rural Thaksin supporters and the elite, although those disparities remain significant and motivate many of the participants. The fight also involves regional rivalries; most of the protesters hail from the northeastern part of Thailand and resent the control emanating from the richer governing class in Bangkok. The differences are also exploited by politicians who are motivated by their own self-interest. Many Puea Thai politicians have attached themselves to Thaksin to win votes but come from the same privileged—and often corrupt—club of powerbrokers as members of the ruling coalition.

The competing protestors are divided between two main groups: the People's Alliance for Democracy (PAD), known as the "yellow shirts" and the United Front for Democracy Against Dictatorship (UDD), known as the "red shirts." The PAD, initially formed under the leadership of media baron Sondhi Limthongkul in early 2006, led large-scale protests accusing Thaksin of corruption and subversion of democratic practices, which some observers claim laid the groundwork for the military coup. The PAD are a mix of the military, royalists, the bureaucracy, and largely urban and middle class citizens. The combination of Thaksin's broad popularity and clampdown on opposition opinions in the media threatened many of those in the "old guard."

The UDD, or "red shirts," are mostly Thaksin loyalists who insist that the current government is illegitimate and demand Thaksin's return. A fundamental divide between the two groups centers on the electoral process, with the yellow shirts arguing that ethical imperatives trump the polls, while the red shirts believe that governance should be determined entirely by the population's vote. Both sides have seen what they perceive as distortion of the system and have taken to the streets with their grievances.

As the crisis exploded into violence in 2010, splinter groups emerged within all of the major institutions: the government, the military, the police, the anti-government "red shirt" protestors, and the "yellow shirt" counter-protestors, who disrupted Bangkok with their own mass rallies in 2008. Rogue elements among the police and military forces and among the protestors' ranks may have been responsible for the most egregious violence and damage that occurred during the stand-off.

Role of the Palace

The apparent reluctance of King Bhumiphol to be involved in the deep conflicts that have torn at Thai society has deepened the uncertainty about the path ahead. The power of the palace, and particularly the intense popularity of the king himself, has traditionally provided an important pillar of stability for Thailand. The king, who has served since 1946, commands tremendous respect and loyalty from the Thai public and has exercised influence over politics throughout his reign. The king, born in 1927, is reportedly in poor health, giving rise to anxiety about succession. In years past when civil unrest spilled over into violence, the king's public interventions had successfully stemmed the conflict. Some leaders on both sides have begun openly questioning the king's ability to be a unifying force, or why he did not appeal for an end to the violence during the most heated street battles.

Due to stringent lèse-majesté laws, under which it is a crime, punishable with a prison term of up to 15 years, to "criticize, insult or threaten" the King, Queen, royal heir apparent, or regent, the issue of royal continuity is rarely broached publicly. According to news reports, the use of these legal provisions has soared in recent years: reportedly, the number of charges brought before the lower courts has risen from five or six a year in the early 2000s to 478 in 2010 and thousands of websites have been blocked.[3] An American was arrested for lèse-majesté in 2011, drawing complaints from the U.S. embassy in Bangkok.

TIMELINE SURROUNDING THAILAND'S TURMOIL

Thaksin's Rise and Fall

The Thai Rak Thai (TRT) party, formed by Thaksin in 1999, benefitted politically from the devastation of the 1997 Asian financial crisis on Thailand's economy, and the subsequent loss of support for the ruling Democrats. Thaksin's platform included a nationalist call for Thais to regain control over their nation (which had been forced into an unpopular International Monetary Fund (IMF) rescue plan in 1997), and populist programs that appealed to a wide cross-section of Thais. Many analysts contended that Thaksin and his party enjoyed power unprecedented in modern Thai politics.[4] In February 2005, the TRT won parliamentary elections outright—a first in Thai politics—and swiftly dropped its former coalition partners to form a single-party government.

Thaksin remained electorally popular, but many criticized his government for human rights abuses, both in the restive south and through an aggressive anti-narcotics campaign that allegedly led to hundreds of extra-judicial killings. He was also accused of intimidating journalists and paying scant attention to Thailand's vibrant NGO sector.

Shortly after TRT's impressive victory, Thaksin's popularity faltered due to a weak economy, corruption scandals involving cabinet members, and his failure to stem violence in the south. In early 2006, large public demonstrations calling for his ouster gained momentum. The protestors, mostly members of the urban, educated class, were reportedly unhappy with his authoritarian style, perceived attacks on the free press, mishandling of the violence in the south, and most of all, the tax-free sale of his family's telecommunications firm to a Singapore state company in a $1.9 billion deal that many suspected was not taxed because of Thaksin's clout.

Widespread protests led Thaksin to call for a new round of parliamentary elections in April 2006. After a less-than-convincing victory by his party in an election boycotted by the opposition, Thaksin resigned, then quickly stepped back into power as a "caretaker" prime minister. After Thailand's king called for the courts to resolve the crisis, the Constitutional Court ruled the elections invalid, and new elections were set for November 2006. Despite widespread discontent with Thaksin among the country's middle class and urban dwellers, Thaksin's strong support in rural areas was expected to propel the TRT to a win in the elections.

Military Coup Ousts Thaksin

On September 19, 2006, with Thaksin visiting New York for the United Nations General Assembly, Royal Thai Army Commander-in-Chief Sonthi Boonyaratglin led a bloodless military coup in Bangkok, ousting Thaksin and declaring martial law. The coup was the 18th since the formation of the constitutional monarchy in 1932, but the first in 15 years. The new leaders formed the Council for Democratic Reform (CDR), later changing the name to the Council for National Security (CNS). King Bhumiphol reportedly endorsed the takeover after it occurred. Under interim Prime Minister Surayud Chulanont, a former Army commander, the ruling military government struggled to establish credibility and legitimacy in the months that followed. A series of economic policy moves unnerved investors.

After the coup, the bureaucratic and military elite—with the royal imprimatur—controlled Thailand, while the political parties appeared marginalized and disorganized. In May 2007, a junta-appointed constitutional tribunal ruled that TRT must disband because it had violated election laws in the April 2006 polls and that Thaksin and 110 party executives were banned from politics for five years. The same day, the court acquitted the opposition Democratic Party of a series of other election violation charges. Many observers criticized the rulings as delaying the return to democracy by disenfranchising the most popular political party in Thailand.

In August 2007, a nation-wide referendum on the constitution drafted by a junta-appointed committee passed narrowly amid tepid turnout. The constitution came under criticism for reversing many of the democratic principles enshrined in the 1997 charter. Under the new constitution, the number of parliamentary seats are reduced, nearly half of the Senate is appointed by a panel of judges and bureaucrats, and the coup leaders are granted amnesty. The document, designed to prevent the re-emergence of a Thaksin-like strongman leader, suggested to some analysts that Thailand may return to a period of weak, unstable coalition governments.

U.S. Response

Following the coup, U.S. officials faced the challenge of expressing disapproval for the rollback of democracy while not sacrificing what many view as a crucial relationship. Many observers saw the response as relatively mild. On September 28, 2006, the U.S. State Department announced the suspension of several assistance programs under Section 508 of the Foreign Operations Appropriations Act (P.L. 109-102): Foreign Military Financing

(FMF, for defense procurement), International Military Education Training funds (IMET, provides training to professionalize the Thai military), and peacekeeping operation programs. Also suspended were funds for counterterrorism and other operations appropriated under Section 1206 of the National Defense Authorization Act for FY2006. The suspended programs totaled over $29 million. Other programs deemed to be in the U.S. interest continued, according to the State Department. After Surayud was appointed, U.S. Ambassador Ralph Boyce was reportedly the first foreign diplomat to meet with him.

On February 6, 2008, the U.S. State Department announced that Deputy Secretary of State John Negroponte had certified to Congress that Thailand had restored a democratically elected government, thereby removing legal restrictions on assistance that had been imposed after the coup. A statement from the U.S. ambassador said that funds were reinstated for programs that include the International Military Exchange Training (IMET) programs, Foreign Military Financing (FMF), and the Global Peacekeeping Operations Initiative (GPOI).

Political Turmoil under Successive Governments

After the coup, an interim military government took power, generally proving to be ineffective at governance but orchestrating relatively clean elections in December 2007. The People's Power Party (PPP), a successor party to Thaksin's Thai Rak Thai (TRT) party, won a strong victory in parliamentary elections, but its two subsequent prime ministers—Samak Sundaravej and Somchai Wongsawat—were both forced to resign because of decisions by Thailand's court system. Thaksin, convicted in absentia of corruption, remained a major presence in Thai politics from exile, appearing via video link to appeal to his supporters. In late 2009, he accepted an economic advisory position from the Cambodian government, infuriating Bangkok officials.

Both sides of the political divide employed massive protests that disrupted Bangkok for months in 2008. Demonstrations by anti-Thaksin forces swelled in number and aggression through the fall of 2008, culminating in a week-long takeover of Bangkok's two major airports late in the year. In December 2008, Abhisit Vejjajiva, leader of the Democrat Party, was elected by the parliament as prime minister by collecting enough defector votes from former PPP lawmakers. The PPP regrouped under the "Puea Thai" or "For Thais" Party.

After the Abhisit government took power, pro-Thaksin groups took to the streets, eventually forcing the embarrassing cancelation of an Asian leaders' summit in April 2009. At times, the demonstrations turned violent, with several deaths on each side. The protests, and particularly the airport takeovers, hurt Thailand's economy, especially the crucial tourism sector. The respective governments in power, however, appeared loath to order a crackdown, which, they may have calculated, would make the situation appear even more volatile and chaotic.

Spring 2010 Violence

Beginning in mid-March 2010, anti-government "Red Shirt" protestors occupied parts of Bangkok for nine weeks. Initially peaceful, the demonstrations and the response from the security forces became increasingly aggressive, eventually spiraling into urban warfare. The initial restraint demonstrated by both sides gave way to the worst political violence in modern Thai history. On May 19, 2010, armored vehicles and infantry troops stormed the protestors' encampments and several protest leaders surrendered. As the crowd retreated, a violent fringe of the movement set fire to dozens of buildings, burning a large shopping mall to the ground and damaging the Thai stock exchange. By the time a military crackdown dispersed the crowds, at least 90 people were dead and up to 2,000 wounded.

July 2011 Elections

Thailand's national elections on July 3, 2011, swept the populist Puea Thai party into power, led by Thaksin's younger sister Yingluck Shinawatra, a political novice who became Thailand's first female prime minister. Although Puea Thai won a majority of seats (265 of the 500), it formed a coalition with several smaller parties to claim an even stronger hold on power and ensure Yingluck's election. After officially taking office, she announced a cabinet that most observers saw as relatively moderate and inoffensive to the establishment powers in Bangkok. Although many analysts had earlier feared that the military would interfere with the political process if a pro-Thaksin government won elections, the army remained in its barracks.

Yingluck faced the challenge of governing a largely divided country, delivering on campaign promises to assist the mostly rural base of her party, and responding to calls for justice from the Red Shirt activists who were involved in the 2010 street protests and support the return of her brother to Thailand. The government outlined its top priorities, including reconciliation following 2010's political violence and increasing the minimum wage. In foreign policy, the government emphasized building stronger relationships with the region, which includes addressing a longstanding conflict with Cambodia surrounding a temple on the Thai-Cambodian border.

In the 2011 elections, Puea Thai soundly defeated the ruling Democrat Party, led by Abhisit Vejjajiva, who had held power since December 2008. The Democrats captured only 159 seats, winning in their traditional strongholds of Bangkok and the south but being soundly defeated in the heavily populated and poorer northern and northeastern parts of the country. Although the Thai economy performed well in 2010, posting nearly 8% growth, the Democrats failed to win over the majority of voters. Street protests persisted through much of Abhisit's tenure, with proThaksin "Red Shirt" protestors demanding the release of the movement's leaders who have been jailed since the outbreak of violence in 2010. Abhisit's government had advanced plans to appeal to the poorer rural voters who had flocked to Thaksin, including more access to loans and assistance, but these efforts didn't earn the government much electoral support. The Democrats also promoted a national reconciliation plan and advocated for reforms that would broaden public participation in the political arena. Abhisit also faced pressure from the "Yellow Shirt" movement, which launched protests calling for more assertive Thai policy on the issue of sovereignty surrounding the disputed Preah Vihear temple on the border with Cambodia.

VIOLENCE IN THE SOUTHERN PROVINCES

Thailand has endured a persistent separatist insurgency in its majority-Muslim southern provinces, which include the provinces of Yala, Narathiwat, Pattani, and—to a lesser extent— Songhkla, while dealing with political instability in its capital. Since January 2004, sectarian violence between insurgents and security forces in Thailand's majority-Muslim provinces has left around nearly 5,000 people dead, according to press reports. The groups that have led this surge in violence are generally poorly understood, and their motives are difficult to characterize. Many believe they are mostly focused on local autonomy, but even the Thai government has a poor understanding of the diverse groups active in the south. The successive governments have taken somewhat different approaches to curbing the violence in the south, but none appear to have found a way to resolve the ongoing insurgency.

Background to the Current Conflict

The southern region has a history of separatist violence, though the major movements were thought to have died out in the early 1990s. Thai Muslims have long expressed grievances for being marginalized and discriminated against, and the area has lagged behind the rest of Thailand in economic development. The recent death toll of over 3,300 includes suspected insurgents killed by security forces, as well as victims of the insurgents. This includes both Buddhist Thais, particularly monks and teachers, and local Muslims.

After a series of apparently coordinated attacks by the insurgents in early 2004, the central government declared martial law in the region. Moreover, a pattern of insurgent attacks—targeted shootings or small bombs that claim a few victims at a time and counterattacks by the security forces—has developed. The pattern crystallized into two major outbreaks of violence in 2004: on April 28, Thai soldiers killed 108 insurgents, including 34 lightly armed gunmen in a historic mosque, after they attempted to storm several military and police outposts in coordinated attacks; and on October 25, 84 local Muslims were killed: 6 shot during an erupting demonstration at the Tak Bai police station and 78 apparently asphyxiated from being piled into trucks after their arrest. The insurgents retaliated with a series of more gruesome killings, including beheadings, following the Tak Bai incident.

Failure of Successive Governments' Approaches

The Thaksin government's handling of the violence was widely criticized as ineffective and inflammatory. Critics charged that the Thaksin government never put forth a sustained strategy to define and address the problem, that it repeatedly and arbitrarily shuffled leadership positions of those charged with overseeing the region, and that it failed to implement adequate coordination between the many security and intelligence services on the ground.

Under the military government, interim Prime Minister Surayud Chulanont took a more conciliatory approach by publicly apologizing to Muslim leaders for past government policies in the south and resurrecting a civilian agency responsible for improving relations between the security forces, the government, and southern Muslims that Thaksin had abolished. General Sonthi Boonyaratglin, leader of the coup and the first Muslim commander of the Army, advocated negotiations with the separatist groups as opposed to the more confrontational strategy pursed by Thaksin. However, the violence increased in the months following the coup.[5] Some analysts said that a younger generation of more radicalized insurgents resisted the more conciliatory approach of the new leadership in Bangkok. Criticism emerged that Surayud's policies were insufficiently implemented, law enforcement was unable to effectively prosecute cases, and that intelligence coordination remained abysmal.

Subsequent governments, under fire from their inceptions, were unable to devote sustained attention to the south. Critics maintain that several of the governments did not focus adequate resources on the area as they struggled to maintain their hold on power in Bangkok. The region remains under martial law, which allows security forces to arrest suspects without warrants and detain them for up to 30 days. Since June 2007, a more concentrated counter-insurgency campaign known as "Operation Southern Protection" led to far more arrests, but many analysts see the mass arrests as fueling local resentment. Observers note an increase in more lethal and bold attacks. Human rights groups have continued to criticize the military for its mistreatment of Muslim suspects; in March 2008, Human Rights Watch accused the army of torturing an arrested Muslim cleric who later died in police custody.[6]

Little Evidence of Transnational Elements

Most regional observers stress that there is no convincing evidence to date of serious Jemaah Islamiyah (JI) involvement in the attacks in the southern provinces, and that the overall long-term goal of the movement in the south remains the creation of an independent state with Islamic governance. Many experts characterize the movement as a confluence of different groups: local separatists, Islamic radicals, organized crime, and corrupt police forces. They stress, however, that sectarian violence involving local Muslim grievances provides a ripe environment for foreign groups to become more engaged in the struggle. Some of the older insurgent organizations earlier were linked to JI, have reportedly received financial support from foreign Islamic groups, and have leaders who have trained in camps in Libya and Afghanistan. The insurgency has at times heightened tensions with Malaysia, as many of the leaders are thought to cross the border fairly easily. Despite these links, foreign elements apparently have not engaged significantly in the violence.

Leadership of Insurgency Unclear

Identifying the groups directing the insurgency has been challenging, but most analysis suggests that there is no one organization with authority over the others. Some reports suggest that the Barisan Revolusi Nasional-Coordinate (BRN-C) has coordinated other groups that operate largely autonomously. Other actors are older Islamist separatist groups, including the Pattani United Liberation Organization (Pulo) and Gerakan Mujahideen Islam Pattani (GMIP). An organization called Bersatu at one point claimed to be an umbrella grouping for all the insurgent factions, but appears to have very limited authority over the disparate networks.

The government's inability to establish an authority with whom to negotiate has limited its ability to resolve the conflict peacefully. In February 2013, Yingluck's government made an effort in this regard, announcing that it would initiate peace talks with the Barisan Revolusi National (BRN), a group whose leaders largely reside outside Thailand. BRN reportedly suspended the talks in August 2013. Had the effort been successful, it is unclear how it would have influenced the actions of groups on the ground.[7]

U.S.-Thailand Security Relations

A Long-Standing Southeast Asian Ally

The 1954 Manila Pact of the former Southeast Asia Treaty Organization (SEATO), together with the 1962 Thanat-Rusk communiqué, forms the basis of the U.S.-Thai security relationship. Although SEATO was dissolved in 1977, Article IV (1) of the Manila Pact, which calls for signatories to "act to meet the common danger" in the event of an attack in the treaty area, remains in force. Thailand has been considered to be one of the major U.S. security allies in East Asia, along with Japan, South Korea, Australia, Singapore, and the Philippines.

The U.S. security relationship with Thailand has a firm historical foundation based on joint efforts in the Korean War, the Vietnam War, and the 1991 Persian Gulf War. Thailand sent more than 6,500 troops to serve in the

United Nations Command during the Korean War, where the Thai force suffered over 1,250 casualties.[8] A decade later, the United States staged bombing raids and rescue missions over North Vietnam and Laos from Thailand. During the Vietnam War, up to 50,000 U.S. troops were based on Thai soil, and U.S. assistance poured into the country to help Thailand fight its own domestic communist insurgency.[9] Thailand also sent troops to South Vietnam and Laos to aid the U.S. effort. The close security ties continued throughout the Cold War, with Thailand serving as a solid anti-Communist ally in the region. More recently, Thai ports and airfields played a crucial role in maintaining the flow of troops, equipment, and supplies to the theater in both the 1991 and 2003 Iraq wars.

In October 2003, President George W. Bush designated Thailand as a "major non-NATO ally," a distinction which allows more access to U.S. foreign aid and military assistance, including credit guarantees for major weapons purchases.[10] An agreement concluded with the United States in July 2001 allows Thailand to purchase advanced medium-range air-to-air missiles for its F-16 fighters, a first for a Southeast Asian state.[11] Thaksin authorized the reopening of the Vietnam-era U.S. airbase in Utapao and a naval base in Sattahip, from which the U.S. military can logistically support forces in Afghanistan and the Middle East. Thailand served as the logistics hub for much of the U.S. and international relief effort after the 2004 Indian Ocean tsunami and the 2008 Cyclone Nargis in Burma. U.S. relief operations by air and sea for the entire region were directed out of Utapao air base and Sattahip naval base.

Impact of the 2006 Coup

The military coup and subsequent suspension of military aid by the United States threatened to derail the strong bilateral defense relationship. Following the reinstatement of aid, Thai and U.S. military officials emphasized their commitment to a smooth resumption of close military ties. Several of the programs listed below were suspended under Section 508 of the Foreign Operations Appropriations Act (P.L. 109-102). In May 2007, the annual "Cobra Gold" multinational military exercises went forward despite the suspension of several other military cooperation programs, and have continued annually since.

Support for U.S. and International Operations

Thailand strengthened its partnership with the United States by contributing troops to two American military operations and the broader war on terrorism after the September 11, 2001, attacks. Thailand sent 130 soldiers, largely engineers, to Afghanistan to participate in the reconstruction phase of Operation Enduring Freedom. Thai forces constructed a runway at Bagram Airbase, provided medical services, and conducted some special forces operations.[12]

Although Thailand remained officially neutral during the U.S.-led invasion of Iraq, it contributed to reconstruction efforts in Iraq by dispatching over 450 troops, including medics and engineers, to the southern city of Karbala. The deployment proved unpopular with the Thai public, particularly after the deaths of two soldiers in December 2003. In spring 2004, Thaksin threatened to withdraw the troops early if the security situation continued to disintegrate and resisted U.S. calls to postpone the withdrawal until after the January 2005 Iraqi elections. The withdrawal was completed in September 2004.

In 2010, Thailand contributed to two international efforts by deploying its military. Two naval ships were sent to assist in the multinational counter-piracy mission in the Gulf of Aden off the coast of Somalia for a four-month tour. In late 2010, Thailand also sent a battalion of troops for peacekeeping operations in Darfur, Sudan.

Thailand reportedly provided a "black site" where U.S. Central Intelligence Agency officials were allowed to secretly hold suspected terrorists. According to press reports, two major Al Qaeda figures captured in Pakistan were flown to Thailand for interrogation by U.S. officials.[13] CIA officials have not confirmed the existence of the site.

Asia Pacific Military Transformation

The U.S. Department of Defense initiative to transform and realign the U.S. military around the globe provides potential opportunities for increased security cooperation with Thailand. Pentagon planners are breaking with the quantitative assurance of keeping 100,000 troops on the ground in East Asia in favor of a more mobile, capability-based force. U.S. military planners have emphasized a "places, not bases" concept in Southeast Asia in which U.S. troops can temporarily use facilities for operations and training, without maintaining a lengthy and costly permanent presence. Facilities used by the U.S. military in Thailand fall under the Pentagon's "cooperative security location" concept, in which countries provide access in exchange for upgrades and aid.[14]

Bilateral Security Cooperation

Security Assistance

The United States has provided funds for the purchase of weapons and equipment to the Thai military through the Foreign Military Financing (FMF) program (see *Table 1*). As a major non-NATO ally, Thailand also qualifies for the Excess Defense Articles (EDA) program, which allows for the transfer of used U.S. naval ships and aircraft.

The United States faces stiff competitors in the foreign military sales market in Thailand, particularly because other countries are more willing to engage in barter trade for agricultural products.

Table 1. U.S.Assistance to Thailand 2007-2014 (thousands of dollars)

Account	FY2007	FY2008	FY2009	FY2010	FY2011	FY2012	FY2013 estimate	FY2014 request
DA	0	0	4,500	6,151	5,051	5,051	4,826	5,051
ESF	990	0	2,500	2,500	0	0	0	0
FMF[a]	0	423	1,600	1,600	1,568	1,187	1,424	988
GH	1,400	1,492	1,500	1,500	1,500	1,500	1,000	0
IMETa	0	1,202	1,459	1,571	1,568	1,318	1,234	1,300
INCLE	900	1,686	1,400	1,740	1,740	1,740	1,740	1,466
NADR	2,100	2,483	2,700	3,300	1,541	1,450	1,152	1,320
Peace Corps	2,144	2,278	2,815	3,064	3,300	3,000	3,100	3,700
Totals	7,534	9,786	15,659	18,362	12,968	12,246	11,376	11,275

Sources: U.S. Department of State; USAID.

Notes: DA = Development Assistance; ESF = Economic Support Funds; FMF = Foreign Military Sales Financing; GH = Global Health; IMET = International Military Education and Training; INCLE = International Narcotics and Law Enforcement; NADR = Nonproliferation, Anti-Terrorism, Demining, & Related.

[a] These programs were suspended on September 28, 2006, under Section 508 of the Foreign Operations Appropriations Act (P.L. 109-102) and resumed on February 6, 2008.

Military Exercises

Training opportunities for U.S. forces in Thailand are considered invaluable by the U.S. military. Thailand and the United States have conducted over 40 joint military exercises a year, including Cobra Gold, the world's largest combined military exercise. For the February 2013 exercises, approximately 13,000 military personnel participated in the exercise. The fully participating nations include Thailand, the United States, Singapore, Japan, South Korea, Indonesia and Malaysia, with observers from several other Asian nations also joining, including, for the first time, military officials from Burma.

Training

Tens of thousands of Thai military officers, including many of those in top leadership positions throughout the services and in the civilian agencies, have received U.S. training under the International Military Education and Training (IMET) program. Designed to enhance the professionalism of foreign militaries as well as improve defense cooperation with the United States, the program is regarded by many as a relatively low-cost, highly effective means to achieve U.S. national security goals.

Intelligence

Intelligence cooperation between Thailand and the United States reportedly increased markedly after the September 11, 2001, attacks, culminating in the establishment of the Counter Terrorism Intelligence Center (known as the CTIC) in 2001. The CTIC, which combines personnel from Thailand's intelligence agency and specialized branches of the military and armed forces, provides a forum for CIA personnel to work closely with their Thai counterparts, sharing facilities and information daily, according to reports from Thai security officials.[15] Close cooperation in tracking Al Qaeda operatives who passed through Thailand reportedly intensified into active pursuit of suspected terrorists following the 9/11 strikes.[16] The most public result of enhanced coordination was the arrest of suspected Jemaah Islamiyah leader Hambali, outside of Bangkok in August 2003. Other intelligence cooperation focuses on counter-narcotics or specialized military intelligence.

Law Enforcement

In 1998, the International Law Enforcement Academy (ILEA) Bangkok was established to provide legal training for officials to combat transnational crime.[17] The center is open to government officials from any Southeast Asian country, with the exception of Burma (Myanmar). ILEA Bangkok aims to enhance law enforcement capabilities in each country, as well as to encourage cross-border cooperation. Instruction for the courses is provided largely by the Royal Thai Police, the Thai Office of the Narcotics Control Board, and various U.S. agencies, including the Diplomatic Security Service, the Federal Bureau of Investigation, the Drug Enforcement Agency (DEA), the Department of Homeland Security, and the Internal Revenue Service.[18]

Counter-Narcotics

Counter-narcotics cooperation between Thailand and the United States has been extensive and pre-dates the foundation of ILEA-Bangkok. Coordination between the DEA and Thailand's law enforcement agencies, in conjunction with a mutual legal assistance treaty and an extradition treaty, has led to many arrests of international drug traffickers. Specialized programs include the establishment of Task Force 399, in which U.S. special forces train Thai units in narcotics interdiction tactics.[19]

U.S.-Thailand Trade and Economic Relations

Thailand's economy has continued to perform strongly during the nation's years of political turmoil. In 2012, Thailand was the 25th largest goods trading partner of the United States, with over \$37 billion in two-way trade. The U.S. goods trade deficit with Thailand was \$15.2 billion in 2012, making up 2.1% of the overall U.S. goods deficit. U.S. foreign direct investment in Thailand was \$11.3 billion in 2011. Negotiations for an FTA with Thailand were launched in 2004 but then suspended in 2006 following the military coup. In 2012, Prime Minister Yingluck expressed interest in joining the multilateral negotiations for the Trans-Pacific Partnership (TPP), but Thailand has taken no further steps since then toward joining the talks.

As a major trading nation and large-scale recipient of foreign direct investment, Thailand's economy depends heavily on its trading and investment partners. Economic relations with the United States are central to Thailand's outward-looking economic strategy. According to the U.S. Commerce Department, U.S. trade with Thailand in 2012 consisted of \$10.9 billion in exports and \$26 billion in imports.[20] Major exports from the United States include integrated circuits, computer parts, semi-conductors, cotton, aircraft parts, electronics, soybeans, and oil. Major imports to the United States include electronics, jewelry, seafood, clothing, furniture, natural rubber, auto parts, and rice.[21] The State Department reports that although Japan is Thailand's biggest trading partner, the United States is Thailand's largest export market.

In order to promote the goal of higher levels of trade and investment, the Department of Commerce's International Trade Administration states that current trade concerns regarding Thailand are intellectual property rights laws and enforcement, concerns addressed through consultations and technical assistance, improvements in Thai customs practices, and lack of transparency and efficiency in the customs regime.[22]

Thailand has aggressively pursued FTAs with countries other than the United States in its campaign to expand trading opportunities. Agreements have been signed with Bahrain, China, Peru, Australia, Japan, India, and New Zealand. Further deals are possible with South Korea, Chile, and the European Union (EU). Thailand has championed ASEAN regionalism, seeing the ASEAN Free Trade Area (AFTA, among ASEAN countries only) as a vehicle for investment-driven integration which will benefit Thailand's outward-oriented growth strategy.[23]

Human Rights and Democracy Concerns

International groups, some Members of Congress, and U.S. officials have criticized Thailand's record on human rights. Thailand has neither signed the United Nations Convention Against Torture nor joined the International Criminal Court. Under the various governments that have led the country during the past 12 years, alleged abuses have ranged from extra-judicial killings and curtailment of the press and non-governmental groups under Thaksin, direct military intervention in the political system in the 2006 coup, curtailment of the freedom of expression under strict lese-majeste laws under subsequent governments, the bloody suppression of demonstrations in 2010, and a poor record on combatting human trafficking throughout. Numerous reports have documented the role of Thai military personnel in violently ending the 2010 protests, in which at least 90 persons were killed.

Throughout the turmoil, the state of Thailand's democracy has become a concern for many observers. Many believed that Thailand's democratic processes had been firmly entrenched in the 1990s through a 1997 constitution that sought to strengthen the stability of elected governments and protect greater levels of human rights. However, the 2006 coup, and then a 2007 constitution that many considered to be a move away from the ideals of the

1997 document, brought questions about whether established power centers had truly accepted the democratic system. Those questions have persisted, and the protesters who have massed in late 2013 have called for a change in Thailand's political system, and threatened to disrupt the February 2014 elections.

Under Thaksin

During Thaksin's rule, detractors consistently voiced concern that his strongman style threatened Thailand's democratic institutions. Charges of cronyism and creeping authoritarianism grew louder as his political power strengthened. Previously independent watchdog agencies reportedly weakened under his watch,[24] and some commentators alleged that Thaksin undermined anticorruption agencies by installing political loyalists to protect the business interests of his family and members of his cabinet—sometimes one and the same, as Thaksin had a record of appointing relatives and friends to prominent posts.[25] Thaksin insisted that political strength enhances development, citing Singapore's economic success and lack of political opposition as a model for Thailand to follow.[26]

Outside groups warned that press freedom was squeezed during Thaksin's rule, documenting multiple cases in which critical journalists and news editors were dismissed, and pointing to a libel suit against an outspoken editor filed by a telecommunications corporation that Thaksin founded.[27] Human Rights Watch claims that Thaksin stifled criticism from the media of his administration's controversial policies, such as the deaths of about 2,500 individuals in the government-sponsored "war on drugs."[28]

Coup and Aftermath

The coup itself raised obvious concerns about the democratic process in Thailand. Much of the Thai press and some long-time Thai watchers embraced the notion that the coup was necessary for Thailand to move forward; that is, that the military coup represented less of a threat to Thai democracy than Thaksin's perceived systematic dismantling of the democratic system. In addition, much of the state's apparatus, including the key institutions of the parliament, the judicial branch, and watchdog agencies, reportedly has been undermined in the past several years. Uncertainty about the king's succession compounded the concern about Thailand's ability to preserve democratic structures and stability in the upcoming years. As political unrest unfolded in recent years, stringent lèse-majesté laws appeared to be applied with more frequency, leading to criticism from free speech advocates.[29] It is a crime, punishable with a prison term of up to 15 years, to "criticize, insult or threaten" the King, Queen, royal heir apparent, or regent. Some groups say this has substantially curtailed freedom of expression.

Trafficking in Persons

Thailand is a source, destination, and transit country for human trafficking victims, according to the State Department. Within Thailand, foreign migrants, particularly from neighboring countries such as Burma, members of ethnic minorities, and stateless persons are at greatest risk of being trafficked for commercial sexual exploitation and for forced labor in seafood-related industries, garment factories, and domestic work. Most victims identified by Thai officials are found in sex trafficking, including children, who are exploited for sex tourism. Children are also reportedly recruited and used by separatist groups to carry out attacks in southern Thailand.

The State Department's 2013 TIP Report described the government of Thailand as not fully in compliance with the minimum standards for the elimination of trafficking. Moreover, the State Department concluded that Thailand has "not shown sufficient evidence" in the past year of efforts to bring itself into compliance. For the 2014 TIP Report, Thailand will be promoted to Tier 2 or downgraded to Tier 3, depending on the State Department's assessment of anti-trafficking progress.

THAILAND IN ASIA

Thailand is important to the region because of its large economy and, until the coup and the civil unrest, its relatively long-standing democratic rule. Southeast Asia is considered by many Asian experts to be a key arena of soft power competition between the United States and China: the loss of a democratic government, as well as any resulting friction with the United States, could be considered an opening for closer Sino-Thai relations.

Strong Ties with China

Sino-Thailand ties, historically far closer than Beijing's relations with most other Southeast Asian states, have continued to strengthen. Bilateral trade and positive relations have boomed over the past decade. Even while reasserting its U.S. alliance under Thaksin, Thailand continued to court China, including inking agreements on technology, environmental protection, and strategic cooperation.

Military-to-military ties increased through both exchanges and arms sales: China exports major weapons and military equipment to Thailand, a practice that originated in the 1980s when both countries supported Cambodian resistance groups, including the Khmer Rouge, against the Vietnamese-installed government in Phnom Penh. Many analysts saw the suspension of several U.S. military programs following the coup as an opportunity for China to expand its influence in the Thai defense establishment. China participated as an observer for the first time in the May 2008 Cobra Gold exercises. Security cooperation has also been stirred by an October 2011 incident in which 13 Chinese soldiers guarding PRC cargo boats were killed in a raid by armed members of a Burmese minority group in a portion of the Mekong River controlled by Thailand. In December 2011, China began limited joint patrols with Thailand, Laos, and Burma along the Mekong, which is increasingly used for trans-border trade.[30]

Trade and investment between Thailand and China have grown as well. Thai companies, many run by ethnic-Chinese families, were among the largest early investors in China following its economic opening in 1979. Thailand has been a strong backer of trade agreements with China. The China-ASEAN Free Trade Agreement (FTA) went into effect in January 2010, and China replaced the United States as Thailand's largest trading partner that year. Thai-PRC trade grew 51% between 2010 and 2012, compared to 24% growth in Thai-U.S. trade.[31]

Thailand's strong relationship with China is based on a history far less antagonistic than Beijing's past with many other ASEAN countries. After the U.S. withdrawal from Vietnam, Bangkok pursued a strategic alignment with Beijing in order to contain Vietnamese influence in neighboring Cambodia. Bangkok restored diplomatic ties with Beijing in 1975, long before other Southeast Asian nations. The sizeable ethnic Chinese population in Thailand assimilated relatively easily and became a strong presence in the business world, and in the political arena as well. Thailand also has no territorial disputes with China in the South China Sea, unlike Vietnam, the Philippines, Malaysia, and Brunei Darussalam. In 2013, it served as ASEAN's coordinator of discussions with China over a potential Code of Conduct for parties in the South China Sea, which brought the restart of these negotiations after several years of stasis.

Thailand-Burma Ties

Thailand has long had a deeply uneasy relationship with Burma's government, both during the period in which Burma was led by a military regime and in the current reform period. Much of the 1,800 kilometer border that separates the two nations has for years been held on the Burmese side by ethnic-minority militias that oppose the central government. The flow of narcotics, migrants, and sometimes militants across the border are some of Thailand's most pressing foreign policy and security problems.

Until the Obama Administration began pursuing an opening with Burma, Bangkok's approach toward Burma had been seen as conflicting with U.S. policy for many years. While the United States pursued strict economic and diplomatic sanctions against the regime, Thailand led ASEAN's "constructive engagement" initiative, which favors integration and incentives to coax Burma into reform.

From Thailand's perspective, the engagement policy served to minimize the danger of a large-scale military struggle and to expand opportunities for Thai business in Burma. Thailand has been criticized for supporting the junta through substantial trade, particularly in natural gas. Thai-Burma trade totaled $6.1 billion in 2011, according to the Bank of Thailand.

During years when the Burmese regime was largely isolated from the international community, this gave Thailand some greater degree of access to the regime. In 2008, for instance, as international groups struggled for access to Burma to provide humanitarian relief following Cyclone Nargis, Burma granted Thai officials and aid workers entry.

In the wake of recent reforms in Burma, Thailand, like much of the region, is assessing whether Burmese reforms are real and sustainable, and seeking to build relationships in the country and encourage the continuation of political reform.

In 2013, Thailand led moves to invite two Burmese Army officers to the multilateral Cobra Gold exercises, and some observers argue that Thailand could take a leadership role in bringing the Burmese military into other regional security initiatives.

Some congressional leaders have criticized Bangkok for its treatment of Burmese refugees, migrant workers, and political dissidents living in Thailand. Backed by human rights groups' reports, some U.S. lawmakers have leveled charges of arrests and intimidation of Burmese political activists, as well as the repatriation of Burmese who seek political asylum.[32] In the past, Congress has passed legislation that provides money to refugees who fled Burma, particularly those in Thailand.[33]

Refugees in Thailand

Thailand has been a magnet for economic and political refugees for many years, particularly from the neighboring countries of Laos, Cambodia, and, most prominently, Burma. Displaced populations of ethnic minorities from Southeast Asia have sought refuge across Thailand's long borders, attracted by relatively loose immigration controls and often lenient treatment by Thai authorities.

The United Nations High Commissioner for Refugees (UNHCR) estimates that over three decades, around 3 million asylum seekers have sought refuge in Thailand, and the Thai government views Burma as presenting the most immediate source of refugee problems. Burmese refugees in Thailand come from a variety of ethnic groups that have fled attacks on their villages by the Burmese army and warlords. Another estimated 200,000 refugees and asylum seekers representing groups (many of them Hmong refugees from Laos) live elsewhere in the country. In addition, Thailand's reputation for relative tolerance for refugees, as well as crackdowns in other recipient countries, has attracted an increasing number of North Korean asylum-seekers. A strong network of international humanitarian organizations exists in Thailand to provide assistance to these populations.

Although Thailand has been generally cooperative in helping Burmese refugees, successive Thai governments have expressed frustration with the continuing presence of refugees and periodically clamped down on the incoming asylum seekers. Thailand's position is that it does not want to become an indefinite host, nor does it want to absorb those Burmese who do not qualify as refugees.

Moreover, the government argues that the camps were intended for temporary use and are not considered suitable for permanent habitation. In the last few years, the Thai government has come under considerable criticism for its refugee treatment. In late 2009, the Thai army deported over 4,300 Hmong refugees back to Laos, where they may face persecution. Although Thai officials deemed the eviction "voluntary," the United Nations was not allowed access to determine their refugee status. Similarly, the Thai military was found to have forcibly pushed boats of Rohingya refugees from Burma out to sea in January 2009.

ASEAN Relations

Thailand's "local" foreign policy with fellow Southeast Asian nations who make up ASEAN (Indonesia, Malaysia, the Philippines, Singapore, Brunei Darussalam, Vietnam, Laos, Burma, and Cambodia) consists of a web of complicated relations. As one of the largest and most economically developed of the ASEAN countries, Thailand has much to gain for promoting ASEAN's significance in global affairs.

With its favorable geographic location and broad-based economy, Thailand has traditionally been considered among the most likely countries to play a major leadership role in Southeast Asia and has been an aggressive advocate of increased economic integration in the region. Bangkok has developed strong relations with its mainland Southeast Asian neighbors through infrastructure assistance and other aid. In turn, Vietnam, Laos, and Cambodia provide raw materials, inexpensive manufacturing, and expanding markets for Thailand. Particularly under Thaksin, Thailand pursued enhanced relations with Singapore based on a common interest in liberalizing trade and with the Philippines centered on a mutual interest in combating terrorism, but those emphases have cooled since Thaksin's departure.

Despite cooperative elements, Bangkok's relations with its neighbors are often characterized by tension and diplomatic spats. Intermittent tension with Cambodia re-ignited in 2008 over competing territorial claims of Preah Vihear, a temple situated along the Thai-Cambodian border and in February 2011, several consecutive days of shelling left at least 10 people dead and prompted calls from Cambodia for the United Nations to intervene. On November 11, 2013, the International Court of Justice ruled that the temple and the area immediately surrounding it were Cambodia's territory. Though Thai and Cambodian troops remain in the area, the ruling has been greeted peacefully.

Relations with Malaysia have been complicated by the insurgency in Thailand's majority-Muslim southern provinces, which border Malaysia. Many Thai Muslims are ethnically Malay and speak Yawi, a Malay dialect, and at times the Malaysian public has grown angry at the perceived violence against Muslims in Thailand.

Thailand and Malaysia have cooperated on efforts to seek talks with separatist groups in the South. However, many separatist leaders reside in northern Malaysia, making the issue a point of concern as the violence continues.

Source: Map Resources. Adapted by CRS.

Figure 1. Map of Thailand.

End Notes

[1] A June 2012 report by the National Bureau for Asian Research concluded: "Although the U.S.-Thailand alliance made a successful transition out of the Cold War framework of the Vietnam War era to a more flexible arrangement, it has stagnated in recent years. This has been caused by domestic distractions on both sides, differences in threat perceptions, and the expansion of both countries' political, economic, and security relations in the region." Catharin Dalpino, Old Alliance for the New Century: Reinvigorating the U.S.-Thailand Alliance. National Bureau for Asian Research. June 8, 2012.

[2] Thaksin in Cambodia: New Year's Partying. The Economist, April 17, 2011.

[3] "Review Thailand's Lese Majeste Laws," TODAY (Singapore), July 22, 2011.

[4] See Ganesan, N. "Thaksin and the Politics of Domestic and Regional Consolidation in Thailand," Contemporary Southeast Asia, vol. 26, no. 1 (April 2004).

[5] "Thailand's Leaders Struggle for Solution as Separatists' Violence Increases," The New York Times. February 26, 2007.

[6] "Thailand: Imam's Killing Highlights Army Abuse in South," from Human Rights Watch webpage at http://www.hrw.org/legacy/english/docs/2008/03/26/thaila18346.htm.

[7] International Crisis Group. Talking and Killing in Southern Thailand. August 9, 2013.

[8] See http://korea50.army.mil/history/factsheets/allied.shtml (official public access website for Department of Defense Commemoration of the 50th anniversary of the Korean War).

[9] The Eagle and the Elephant: Thai-American Relations Since 1833 (Bangkok: U.S. Agency for International Development, 1997).

[10] Under section 517 of the Foreign Assistance Act of 1961, the President can designate a non-North Atlantic Treaty Organization state as a major ally for the purposes of the Foreign Assistance Act and the Arms Export Control Act.

[11] Limaye, Satu P. "Minding the Gaps: The Bush Administration and U.S.-Southeast Asia," Contemporary Southeast Asia, vol. 26, no. 1 (April 2004).

[12] "Thai Soldiers Help Rebuild Afghanistan," The Nation (Thailand), July 4, 2003.

[13] "CIA Operates Secret Prisons Outside U.S.," Wall Street Journal Asia. November 2, 2005.

[14] Kaplan, Robert D., "How We Would Fight China," The Atlantic Monthly. June 2005.

[15] Crispin, Shawn, and Leslie Lopez, "U.S. and Thai Agents Collaborate in Secret—Cold-War-Style Alliance Strikes Jemaah Islamiyah Where It Least Expects It." Asian Wall Street Journal, October 1, 2003.

[16] Ibid.

[17] ILEA-Bangkok is one of four ILEAs in the world. The others are located in Hungary, Botswana, and Roswell, New Mexico.

[18] Course information from http://www.ileabangkok.com.

[19] Chambers, Paul, "U.S.-Thai Relations After 9/11: A New Era in Cooperation?" Contemporary Southeast Asia, Vol. 26, Issue 3. December 2004.

[20] International Trade Administration, U.S. Commerce Department, accessed at http://tse.export.gov/TSE/ MapDisplay.aspx.

[21] Office of Commercial Thailand Affairs, Royal Thailand Embassy, 2007.

[22] "U.S.-Thailand Trade Relations," International Trade Administration, U.S. Department of Commerce, September 2007.

[23] Chirathivat, Suthiphand, and Sothitorn Mallikamas, "Thailand's FTA Strategy: Current Developments and Future Challenges," ASEAN Economic Bulletin, vol. 21, no. 1 (April 2004).

[24] "Thaksin's Way-Thailand's Election," The Economist. February 5, 2005.

[25] "Thailand Risk: Alert—Corruption May Still Go Unchecked," Economist Intelligence Unit, July 19, 2004.

[26] "One Party Rule: Opposition Does Not Need to Be Strong, Says PM," The Nation (Bangkok), August 10, 2004.

[27] "Rights Group Says Libel Suit Deepens Assault on Thailand's Media," Agence France Press, August 31, 2004.

[28] "Thailand: Libel Suit Deepens Assault on the Press," Human Rights Watch. September 1, 2004.

[29] "Thai Officials Move to Quash Dissent in Book, Newspaper," Washington Post. March 26, 2009.

[30] "China Deploys Patrols Along the Mekong," Wall Street Journal, December 11, 2011.

[31] Source text missing.

[32] See Out of Sight, Out of Mind: Thai Policy Toward Burmese Refugees and Migrants, Human Rights Watch Report, released February 2004. Also Abandoned on Arrival, Senate Foreign Relations Committee report on the treatment of Burmese refugees in Malaysia and Thailand.

[33] H.R. 4818, Foreign Operations Appropriations, Section II, Bilateral Assistance.

In: Thailand
Editor: Kenny N. Cade

ISBN: 978-1-63117-596-1

Chapter 2

THAILAND 2012 HUMAN RIGHTS REPORT*

U.S. Department of State; Bureau of Democracy, Human Rights and Labor

EXECUTIVE SUMMARY

Thailand is a constitutional monarchy with a revered king who has traditionally exerted strong influence. A coalition government led by Yingluck Shinawatra and her Puea Thai (For Thais) Party came to power in August 2011 following national elections in July for the National Assembly lower house that were generally viewed as free and fair. Security forces reported to civilian authorities.

The most persistent human rights problems included abuses by government security forces and local defense volunteers in the context of the continuing Muslim separatist insurgency in the South; the continued reported use at times of excessive force by security forces, including police killing, torturing, and otherwise abusing criminal suspects, detainees, and prisoners; and continued government limits on freedom of speech and press.

Other human rights problems included continued poor, overcrowded, and unsanitary prison and detention facilities; occasional arbitrary arrests and detention; government limits on freedom of assembly; insufficient protection for vulnerable populations, including refugees; violence and discrimination

* This is an edited, reformatted and augmented version of a report released by the U.S. Department of State; Bureau of Democracy, Human Rights and Labor, dated April 2013.

against women; sex tourism; sexual exploitation of children; trafficking in persons; discrimination against persons with disabilities, minorities, hill tribe members, and foreign migrant workers; child labor; and some limitations on worker rights.

Authorities occasionally dismissed, arrested, prosecuted, and convicted security force members who committed abusive behavior, but official impunity continued to be a serious problem, especially in provinces where the 2005 Emergency Decree, the 2008 Internal Security Act, and martial law remained invoked.

In the southernmost provinces, the great majority of victims of the violence associated with the separatist insurgency were civilians not taking an active part in hostilities.

SECTION 1. RESPECT FOR THE INTEGRITY OF THE PERSON, INCLUDING FREEDOM FROM:

a. Arbitrary or Unlawful Deprivation of Life

There were continued reports that security forces at times used excessive and lethal force against criminal suspects and committed or were connected to extrajudicial, arbitrary, and unlawful killings. According to the Ministry of Interior's Investigation and Legal Affairs Bureau, security forces--including police, military, and other agencies--killed 109 suspects during the arrest process between October 2011 and September 2012, more than a 50 percent increase compared with 72 suspects killed in the previous corresponding period. The police department with jurisdiction over the location of the killings investigated each case, although no details were available. For example, authorities charged three members of an antidrug unit of the 42nd Border Patrol Police Subdivision, Nakhon Si Thammarat Province, with shooting and killing Sopha Piboon on March 30 as she rode in a vehicle that did not stop when signaled by armed plainclothes officers. Investigations by the Department of Special Investigations and the National Human Rights Commission (NHRC) continued at year's end.

There were no reported developments in the police investigation of the April 2011 killing of two suspected illegal loggers and the injuring of six by Royal Thai Army (RTA) soldiers and forestry officials in Phrae Province, and the investigation continued at year's end.

On July 30, the Bangkok Criminal Court convicted five Kalasin City police officers of murder, concealment of crime, and abuse of power for the 2004 killing of Kiattisak Thitboonkhrong during the government's war on drugs. The court acquitted one person and sentenced three police senior sergeants major (Angkhan Khammoonna, Sutthinan Nonthing, and Phansin Uppananrgeant) to death, Police Lieutenant Colonel Sumit Nunsathit to life imprisonment, and Police Colonel Montri Boonlue to seven years' imprisonment. The court also reportedly allowed the convicted individuals to remain free on bail during their appeals, which continued at year's end, and terminated witness protection services at the time of the verdict.

While there were no confirmed reports that the government or its agents committed politically motivated killings during the year, there were at least five deaths linked to attacks suspected of being politically motivated. For example, two political canvassers were shot and killed while riding home from campaign events: Supphakit Sitthiwilai (Puea Thai Party) on March 5 and Phiraphan Thammaphet (Democrat Party) on May 19.

The trial of two defendants (Ekkachai Pomphadet and Trakun Thongthip) continued at year's end in the case of the June 2011 shooting and killing of Suban Chirapanvanit, a major Bhum Jai Thai Party canvasser and aide to the de facto party leader, and his wife in Bangkok in what was widely believed to be a politically motivated incident. Further police investigation also continued.

Police made no progress in their investigation of the killing of Chutidet Suwannakoet, a political canvasser, near Bangkok in December 2011.

There were reports of killings during the year in connection with the conflict in the southernmost provinces (see section 1.g.).

On September 17, the Truth for Reconciliation Commission of Thailand (TRCT) released the final report of its investigation into the 2010 clashes between security forces and antigovernment protesters in Bangkok and the Northeast that resulted in the deaths of 79 civilians, 11 security force members, and two foreign journalists. The report assigned blame to many parties, including protesters, the government and its security forces, the administration of former prime minister Thaksin Shinawatra, and the military that ousted him in the 2006 coup.

Also on September 17, the criminal court found, in the first of 36 inquests into protest-related deaths, that government authorities killed protester Phan Khamkong. On December 13, the Department of Special Investigations filed charges for the killing of Phan Khamkong against both Abhisit Vejjajiva, Democrat Party member and opposition leader of the lower house, in his former capacity of prime minister, and Suthep Thaugsuban, a Democrat Party member of the lower house, in his former capacities of deputy prime minister and director of the Center for the Resolution of Emergency Situations. The department director announced that the department would not file charges against the soldiers who shot and killed individuals as part of the government's response to protests, since it found they acted in accordance with prime/deputy prime ministerial orders. The defendants, the first government officials so charged, claimed the charges were politically motivated. By year's end there were three more inquest findings of protest-related deaths caused by security forces, and the department announced plans to charge Abhisit and Suthep with those killings during the next parliamentary break scheduled for April 2013. Although it remained unclear at year's end how many others were killed by security forces, armed factions associated with the protests, or accidentally, Abhisit and Suthep faced another 32 or more murder charges and up to 2,000 attempted murder and assault charges.

Via cabinet resolutions of January 10 and March 6, the government created a compensation fund for victims of political violence during the period from 2005 to May 2010 with two billion baht (approximately $65 million) to be administered by the Ministry of Social Development and Human Security (MSDHS). As of August approximately 5,800 individuals registered as "affected persons," and the ministry paid more than 1,800 claims, ranging from 200,000 baht ($6,500) to 7.9 million baht ($258,000), for a total of more than 1.5 billion baht ($49 million) paid.

In addition, via cabinet resolutions of April 24 and August 14, the government created a compensation fund for victims of violence in the South since January 2004, allocating 2.08 billion baht ($68 million) for administration by the Southern Border Provinces Administration Center. As of August it paid more than 3,300 claims, ranging from 500,000 baht ($16,400) to 7.5 million baht ($245,000), for a total of more than 878 million baht ($29 million).

On September 20, the Pattani Provincial Court's postmortem inquest ruled that the 2010 death at the Inkhayuthboriharn Army Camp of Sulaiman Naesa, whose body reportedly showed signs of torture, was a suicide. His family dropped all related civil cases after receiving an award of 7.5 million baht ($245,000) from the southern violence compensation program.

There continued to be several clashes reported between Thai security forces and illegal cross-border loggers throughout the year. Most occurred in Sisaket Province and involved Cambodian citizens. For example, at least two Cambodians were reportedly killed and eight captured in three separate incidents in border areas of Sisaket Province in February alone.

In contrast with 2011, there were no clashes reported between Thai and Cambodian security forces in the disputed border area near the Preah Vihear temple. On July 18, border patrol police began replacing RTA troops in accordance with July 2011 International Court of Justice provisional measures and a bilateral agreement.

b. Disappearance

There were no confirmed reports of politically motivated disappearances, although as of September a nongovernmental organization (NGO) sympathetic to the cause of antigovernment protesters reported that the whereabouts of up to eight individuals remained unknown following their dispersal in 2010 (see also section 1.g., Abductions).

At year's end the National Counter-Corruption Commission (NCCC) continued its investigation into the 2004 disappearance of Muslim attorney and human rights activist Somchai Neelaphaijit. There were also no known developments in the reportedly related August 2011 killing of Jehrohanee Yusoh, the wife of Abduloh Abukaree, a key witness in the Department of Special Investigations case connected to the 2009 disappearance of Somchai Neelaphaijit.

On January 9, the government signed the International Convention for the Protection of All Persons from Enforced Disappearance.

The visit of the UN Working Group on Enforced or Involuntary Disappearances, requested in June 2011, was not arranged by year's end.

c. Torture and Other Cruel, Inhuman, or Degrading Treatment or Punishment

The constitution prohibits such practices. There is no law that specifically prohibits torture, although it is punishable as an offense against the person. Additionally, Section 17 of the Emergency Decree on Public Administration in the State of Emergency (2005), hereinafter "the Emergency Decree," effectively provides immunity from prosecution to security officials for actions committed during the performance of their duties. As of year's end, the cabinet had renewed the Emergency Decree 30 times for consecutive three-month periods since 2005 in several provinces in the South.

Credible NGOs and legal entities continued to report that police and military members occasionally tortured and beat suspects to obtain confessions, and newspapers continued to report numerous cases of citizens accusing police and other security officials of brutality. As remedies during the year, the Songkhla Administrative Court ordered the Internal Security Operations Command (ISOC), the military command responsible for security in the South, to pay compensation for incidents of physical abuse/excessive force by soldiers in 2008 and 2009 in Narathiwat and Yala provinces. An army court levied a six months' suspended sentence and a fine of 2,000 baht ($65) against a soldier for use of excessive force. There also were criminal actions pursued against Royal Thai Police (RTP) officers; available official statistics showed 211 such charges filed from May to December. There were 7,024 internal investigations of official misconduct conducted from October 2010 through September 2011.

A 2010 NHRC report found that torture occurred widely and systematically in the southernmost provinces and that state officials widely used beating and intimidation tactics. Most of the abusers were members of the armed forces or police who arrested and detained suspects under special laws. A follow-up report in February added 23 new abuse cases from the 2004-11 period and submitted them to the agencies involved--the armed forces, police, and Interior Ministry. Although the NHRC received no direct responses to these reports, it noted better agency awareness of human rights requirements, cooperation with NHRC visits and information requests, and agreements to allow regular monitoring of detention operations in the southernmost provinces.

Of the seven cases of alleged brutality against suspected southern Muslim militants by RTA Task Force 38 in Narathiwat Province that two prominent NGOs filed in early 2011, authorities released six individuals without charge in February 2011 and authorized bail for the seventh. There were no further developments in 2012.

The government agreed to schedule in 2014 the visit requested in September 2011 by the UN special rapporteur on torture and other cruel, inhumane, or degrading treatment or punishment.

The appeal by Suderueman Malae, a 2004 torture victim, of his August 2011 Bangkok Criminal Court conviction for maliciously giving false information to inquiry officers and his sentence of two years' imprisonment, continued at year's end. After he reportedly failed to appear for a hearing on December 3 in a similar defamation case filed by Police General Phanuphong Singhara Na Ayutthaya, the court issued a new arrest warrant. Suderueman was a client of disappeared attorney and human rights activist Somchai Neelaphaijit (see section 1.b.) and claimed that Police Major General Chakthip Chaijinda had been involved in his torture and the torture of others.

Prison and Detention Center Conditions

Conditions in prisons and various detention centers--including drug rehabilitation facilities and immigration detention centers (IDCs) where refugees and asylum seekers were detained--remained poor, and most were overcrowded.

Physical Conditions

As of December 1, there were approximately 248,000 prisoners held in prisons and detention facilities with a maximum design capacity of 209,000. About 15 percent were female, and fewer than 1 percent were juveniles. At the IDC in Bangkok, as of August, authorities detained 38 asylum seekers, primarily ethnic Hmong from Vietnam, as well as 17 refugees, mostly from Sri Lanka. In some prisons, sleeping accommodations were insufficient, the lack of medical care was a serious problem, and communicable diseases were widespread. Prisoners generally had access to potable water supplied as tap water treated by water purification. Authorities at times transferred seriously ill prisoners and detainees to provincial or state hospitals.

More than 27 percent of the prison population consisted of pretrial detainees who were not segregated from the general prison population, although those detained under the Emergency Decree in the southernmost provinces often were held in military camps or police stations rather than prisons. Authorities occasionally held men, women, and children together in police station cells pending indictment. Separate detention facilities for juvenile offenders were available in all provinces. Conditions for women were typically better than for men, in large part because the prisoners themselves managed and implemented much of the prison's maintenance and cleaning.

In IDCs, however, authorities detained women and men together and placed juveniles above age 14 with adults. Complaints, especially by Muslim detainees, continued of inadequate and culturally inappropriate food. There also were persistent reports of forced labor and extortion by guards and poor facility ventilation. IDC operators reportedly did not permit detainees, including children, to exercise sufficiently at some facilities.

According to the Ministry of Interior Investigation and Legal Affairs Bureau, 1,026 persons died in official custody from October 2011 to September 2012. Authorities attributed most of those deaths to natural causes.

On May 8, 61-yearold Amphon Tangnopphakun (nicknamed "Uncle SMS") died in prison of apparent natural causes after a court denied bail and imposed a 20-year sentence in November 2011--reportedly the lengthiest such sentence ever--for sending four text messages found to be disrespectful of the queen. Additionally, an investigation continued at year's end into the July 21 death of Kamnung Phonphruk, a murder suspect detained in Phang Nga Provincial Prison. There were no reports of officials killing prisoners during the year until December 30, when police shot and killed two prisoners who had killed a guard taken hostage during their attempted escape from Khao Bin Prison.

Administration

Prison authorities sometimes used solitary confinement of not more than one month, as permitted by law, to punish male prisoners who consistently violated prison rules or regulations; the Department of Corrections maintained that the average confinement was approximately seven days. Authorities also used heavy leg irons to control prisoners who were deemed escape risks or possibly dangerous to other prisoners.

Prisoners and detainees had access to visitors and were permitted religious observance. Authorities permitted prisoners and detainees or their representatives to submit complaints without censorship to ombudsmen but not directly to judicial authorities. Ombudsmen in turn may consider and investigate complaints and petitions received from prisoners and provide recommendations to the Department of Corrections, but they are not empowered to act on a prisoner's behalf, nor may they involve themselves in a case unless an official complaint is received (see also section 5). Authorities rarely investigated complaints and did not make public the results of such investigations.

Prisoner recordkeeping improved during the year with the introduction of an online data-sharing system. However, officials sometimes had to send information through letters and phone calls if data entry was improper. In IDCs, according to independent human rights observers, detainees and their children may be held for years unless they pay a fine and their way home, since by law, "...the alien will have to pay the expense of deportation...[and] [t]he expense of detention shall be charged to the alien's account."

Judicial authorities often imposed alternative penalties (e.g., probation, suspended sentence, fine, or restriction on movement) rather than imprisonment on nonviolent offenders, minors, and convicts with disabilities.

IDCs, administered by the Immigration Police Bureau, which reports to the RTP, were not subject to many of the regulations that govern the regular prison system.

Monitoring

The Ministry of Justice, through its Department of Corrections, is responsible for monitoring prison and detention facility conditions. The government permitted visits to prisons and IDCs by independent human rights observers, and human rights organization representatives were allowed to meet prisoners without third parties present, made repeated visits, and received access to all police facilities in the southernmost provinces. Representatives of a credible, neutral human rights organization reported that authorities allowed access to all prisons in the country during the year and continued to engage with military and police agencies regarding international policing standards and the exercise of police powers.

Representatives of the Office of the UN High Commissioner for Refugees (UNHCR) had access to some detainees at the Suvarnabhumi Airport IDC in Bangkok, but access varied on a case-by-case basis. UNHCR officials were able to interview detainees in the Suan Phlu IDC, and access continued for third countries to process recognized refugees for resettlement.

Separately, individuals who use drugs may be detained in compulsory rehabilitation centers in military camps (there were approximately 86 such centers in 2011) in order to convert drug addicts into "decent citizens." The law classifies drug users as patients rather than criminals, but in practice local authorities made no individual clinical assessments of the severity of drug dependence and afforded no due process before detention. After release, patients were typically not offered follow-up treatment. Media reports catalogued abuses of addict detainees, including physical abuse, and the absence of some health services, such as medically assisted detoxification; HIV prevention, treatment, care, and support; and evidence-based drug dependence treatment. The individuals operating rehabilitation centers were generally military personnel with no medical background. Moreover, civil society groups operating harm-reduction programs faced barriers to delivering their services to drug users, and there continued to be reports that law enforcement officers arrested and harassed outreach workers acting within this government-approved project.

d. Arbitrary Arrest or Detention

The constitution specifically prohibits arbitrary arrest and detention, although government forces occasionally arrested and detained persons arbitrarily. The Emergency Decree, which gives the government authority to detain persons without charge for up to 30 days in unofficial places of detention, remained in effect in the three southern provinces of Yala, Narathiwat, and Pattani (except the Mae Lan District of Pattani Province, as described in section 1.d., Role of the Police and Security Apparatus). The decree, which continued in 31 border-region and southernmost provinces, is in addition to martial law and allows for detention without charge for a maximum of seven days.

Emergency Decree provisions make it very difficult to challenge a detention before a court. Under the decree detainees should have access to legal counsel, but in practice there was no assurance of prompt access to counsel or family members, nor were there transparent safeguards against the mistreatment of detainees. Additionally, the decree effectively provides broad-based immunity from criminal, civil, and disciplinary liability for officials acting under its provisions.

According to an advocacy group, as of December, 16 protesters jailed after the 2010 United Front for Democracy Against Dictatorship (UDD or "Red Shirts") protests remained in pretrial detention, charged with protest-related crimes such as rioting and arson. Lawyers affiliated with the UDD movement continued to pursue bail for these remaining detainees held in several provinces. According to a UDD-affiliated information center, of the 1,857 arrests related to the 2010 protests, authorities prosecuted 1,664 individuals as of December, and the courts dismissed 91 cases, sentenced 850 individuals to probation and/or fines, and imprisoned 220 for less than one year, 63 for one to three years, 10 for three to five years, 10 for five to 10 years, and 27 for more than 10 years. According to the Department of Special Investigations, of the 270 protest-related cases under its jurisdiction, it completed 216 investigations as of December, and trials in 62 cases continued at year's end.

Role of the Police and Security Apparatus

The RTP have the authority to minimize threats to internal security and suppress criminal activity. It is under the direct supervision of the prime minister and a 20- member police commission. The prime minister appoints the police commissioner general subject to cabinet and royal approval. The

Border Patrol Police have special authority and responsibility in border areas to combat insurgent or separatist movements.

The Internal Security Act (ISA) created the ISOC as a state agency under the command of the prime minster, who acts as ISOC director. The ISOC is an interagency monitoring body with both civilian and military representation. The ISA also authorizes broad powers for the military. During the year the government continued its 2011 pilot program in Mae Lan District, Pattani Province, in which it maintained the ISA and martial law without using the Emergency Decree, to study the effectiveness of the ISA alone in maintaining security and decreasing violence in the South. The experiment resulted in a similar or reduced incidence of violence in the district, which is small and historically has had a low incidence of violence compared with the region. An additional four districts in Songkhla Province were under both the ISA and the Emergency Decree. The decree provides the government greater powers than the ISA and therefore takes precedence.

The government lifted the ISA in Bangkok in May 2011, but reimposed it during the November 22-26 period in three Bangkok districts to control the November 24 antigovernment political rally by the Pitak Siam (Protect Siam) group. The demonstration resulted in 68 injuries (15 serious), including several members of the police and press, and 138 arrests of demonstrators, 137 of whom were released the following day without charge. The investigation of a truck driver who rammed a police checkpoint and injured several police officers continued at year's end. Human rights organizations and academics criticized the government for using the ISA to respond to alleged threats to national security by restricting fundamental rights.

There were reports that police abused prisoners and detainees, generally with impunity. Complaints of police abuse may be filed directly with the superior of the accused police officer, the Office of the Inspector General, or the police commissioner general. The NHRC, the Lawyers' Council of Thailand (LCT), the NCCC, the Supreme Court of Justice, the Justice Ministry, and the Office of the Prime Minister also accepted complaints of police abuse and corruption, as did the Office of the Ombudsman. The NHRC received 55 complaints of police abuse during the year.

When police receive a complaint, an internal investigation committee first takes up the matter and may temporarily suspend the officer involved in the complaint during the investigation. Various administrative penalties exist, and serious cases may be referred to a criminal court.

At year's end the joint NCCC-Office of the Attorney General (OAG) committee investigation into the 2009 attempted killing of Sondhi

Limthongkul, a People's Alliance for Democracy leader, continued without reported developments, and the police officer and two soldiers for whom authorities issued arrest warrants remained at large.

Procedures for investigating suspicious deaths, including deaths occurring in police custody, require that a prosecutor, forensic pathologist, and local administrator participate in the investigation and that, in most cases, family members have legal representation at the inquests. However, these procedures often were not followed. Families rarely took advantage of a provision of law that allows them to sue police for criminal action during arrests.

Under a cabinet mandate, the Ministry of Defense requires that service members receive human rights training. Routine training occurred at various levels, including for officers, noncommissioned officers, enlisted personnel, and recruits. Additionally, military service members deploying in support of counterinsurgency operations in the South also received specific human rights training, including training for detailed, situation-specific contingencies.

Arrest Procedures and Treatment While in Detention

With few exceptions the law requires police to obtain a warrant from a judge prior to making an arrest. The system for issuing arrest warrants was subject to misuse by police as well as a judicial tendency automatically to approve all requests for warrants. By law authorities must inform persons of likely charges against them immediately after arrest and allow them to inform someone of their arrest. The law provides for access to counsel for criminal detainees; however, lawyers and human rights groups claimed that police often conducted interrogations without providing access to an attorney. In the southernmost provinces, lawyers reported that under the Emergency Decree they were denied adequate access to detained clients, and some individuals reported they were denied permission to visit detained family members. Authorities sometimes pressured foreign detainees, especially migrant workers and those in the country illegally, to sign confessions without the benefit of a competent interpreter/translator. The Justice Ministry and OAG were authorized to provide an attorney to indigent detainees at public expense, but there were no definitive data available as to such provision. Lawyers noted that fees offered for such service were often low.

The law provides defendants the right to request bail, and the government generally respected this right. However, some human rights groups continued to report that police frequently did not inform detained suspects of their right to request bail or refused to recommend bail after a request was submitted, particularly in drug arrests and cases involving violence in the southernmost provinces.

Arbitrary Arrest

Under martial law the military has the authority to detain persons without charge for a maximum of seven days, and under the Emergency Decree, authorities may detain a person for up to 30 days without charge. For example, on May 31, the military arrested Aliyas Sama-ae and Suekree Teh, Rajabhat Yala University students, and Nuraman Dorloh, a former student activist with the Southern Border Provinces Student Federation, in Yala Province in connection with a bomb incident there. On June 1, authorities released Aliyas and Suekree after interrogation; they detained Nuraman until June 19, when the Yala Provincial Court denied a military request to extend precharge detention and ordered his release (see also section 1.g. concerning conflict-related abuses).

Pretrial Detention

Under normal conditions the law allows police to detain criminal suspects for 48 hours after arrest for investigation. Lawyers reported that police rarely brought cases to court within that 48-hour period. Laws and regulations place offenses for which the maximum penalty is less than three years under the jurisdiction of the district courts, which have different procedures requiring police to submit cases to public prosecutors within 72 hours of arrest. According to the LCT, pretrial detention of criminal suspects for up to 60 days was not uncommon.

Before charging and trial, authorities may detain individuals for a total of 84 days (for the most serious offenses), with a judicial review required for each seven-day period. After formal charge and throughout trial, depending on prosecution and defense readiness, court caseload, and the nature of the evidence, detention may last for one to two years before a verdict and up to six years until Supreme Court appellate review. The time a defendant spent in detention prior to sentencing occasionally equaled or exceeded the sentence for the alleged crime.

Detention of Rejected Asylum Seekers or Stateless Persons

Authorities detained unsuccessful asylum applicants pending deportation and stateless persons. NGOs alleged that detentions were protracted and detention conditions failed to meet satisfactory standards.

Amnesty

A July 10 royal pardon allowed the release of dual-national Joe Gordon (also known as Lerpong Wichaikhammat), who was sentenced in December 2011 to two and one-half years' in prison for lese-majeste offenses. On August 16, a mass pardon in honor of the birthdays of the crown prince (July 28) and the queen (August 12) led to the release of approximately 30,000 prisoners. On August 24, in honor of the queen's birthday, Suchart Narkbangsai and Suriyan Kokpuai, who were both serving three-year sentences for lese-majeste convictions, received royal pardons and were released.

e. Denial of Fair Public Trial

The constitution provides for an independent judiciary. Although the judiciary generally was regarded as independent, it was subject to corruption and outside influence. According to human rights groups, the lack of progress in several high-profile cases involving alleged police and military abuse continued to diminish public trust in the justice system and discourage some victims of human rights abuses (or their families) from seeking justice.

Trial Procedures

The law provides for the presumption of innocence. There is no trial by jury. A single judge decides trials for misdemeanors; two or more judges are required for more serious cases. The constitution provides for a prompt trial, although a large backlog of cases remained in the court system. While most trials are public, the court may order a closed trial, particularly in cases involving national security, the royal family, children, or sexual abuse.

In ordinary criminal courts, defendants enjoy a broad range of legal rights, including access to a lawyer of their choosing, prompt and detailed information of the charges (including no-cost interpretation if needed), and adequate time and facilities to prepare a defense. They also have the rights not to be compelled to testify or confess guilt, to confront witnesses, and to present witnesses. However, indigent defendants were not automatically provided with counsel at public expense, and there were allegations that in practice defendants were not always afforded all the above rights, especially in small or remote provinces.

Legal aid often was provided on an intermittent, voluntary basis and was of low quality. The LCT budget was reduced by more than 12 percent from 2011 to approximately 50 million baht ($1.6 million), following a similar decrease from 2010. Some NGOs reported that legal aid lawyers pressured their clients into paying additional fees directly to them, but the LCT's Lawyer Etiquette Division explained that clients must pay expenses, such as travel, incurred by their attorney.

The court is required to appoint an attorney in cases where the defendant disputes the charges, is indigent, or is a minor, as well as in cases where the possible punishment is more than five years' imprisonment or death. Most free legal aid came from private groups, including the LCT and the Thai Women Lawyers Association. There is no discovery process; consequently, lawyers and defendants do not have access to evidence prior to trial. The law provides for access to courts or administrative bodies to appeal or seek redress, and the government generally respected this right.

Several NGOs continued to express concern over the lack of adequate protection for witnesses, particularly in cases involving alleged police wrongdoing (see section 1.a.). The Justice Ministry Office of Witness Protection had limited resources and primarily played a coordinating role. In most cases witness protection was provided by police, but six other state agencies also participated in the program--the Ministry of Defense; the Office of the Narcotic Control Board; and the Departments of Special Investigations, Provincial Administration, Juvenile Observation and Protection, and Corrections.

Political Prisoners and Detainees

There were no government reports of political prisoners or detainees; however, sources estimated that seven to 18 persons remained detained under lese-majeste laws that outlaw criticism of the monarchy (see section 2.a.). Some of those cases involved persons exercising their rights of freedom of expression and peaceful assembly.

Civil Judicial Procedures and Remedies

There is an independent and impartial judiciary in civil matters. The law provides for access to courts and administrative bodies to sue for damages for, or cessation of, a human rights violation, and the government generally respected this right. However, the Emergency Decree in force in three provinces expressly excludes Administrative Court scrutiny or civil or criminal proceedings against government officials, although victims may seek compensation from a government agency instead.

f. Arbitrary Interference with Privacy, Family, Home, or Correspondence

The constitution specifically prohibits such actions, and the government generally respected these prohibitions. However, martial law and the Emergency Decree give government security forces authority to conduct warrantless searches, and this authority continued to be used routinely in the southernmost provinces and border areas. There were complaints during the year from persons claiming that security forces abused this authority, although the seriousness of allegations declined compared with prior years.

Security services monitored persons, including foreign visitors, who espoused extremist or highly controversial views.

g. Use of Excessive Force and Other Abuses in Internal Conflicts

Internal conflict continued in the ethnic Malay, Muslim-majority, southernmost provinces (Narathiwat, Pattani, Yala, and portions of Songkhla) throughout the year. As a result of frequent bombings and other attacks by suspected insurgents as well as government security operations, tension between the local ethnic Malay Muslim and ethnic Thai Buddhist communities remained high, alongside the local population's persistent distrust of security officials. The Emergency Decree in effect in this southern area gives military, police, and civilian authorities significant powers to restrict certain basic rights and delegates certain internal security powers to the armed forces. The decree also provides security forces broad immunity from prosecution. Moreover, martial law--imposed in 2006-- remained in effect and significantly empowered security forces in Narathiwat, Pattani, and Yala provinces (see also section 1.d. concerning a pilot project).

Killings

Human rights groups accused government forces of extrajudicial killings of individuals suspected of involvement with separatists. For example, on January 29, paramilitary members of Ranger Company 4302 fired on villagers in Nongchik District, Pattani Province, killing four and injuring five. Authorities arrested four members of the Ranger Company, and police and the public prosecutor continued the investigation at year's end to determine appropriate charges. A judicial inquest began on December 23 and continued at year's end. It heard testimony that the incident involved villagers traveling to a funeral who were stopped at a military checkpoint.

According to statistics from the NGO Deep South Watch, separatist violence resulted in 476 individuals killed and 1,349 injured in 1,184 incidents during the year, comparable to 2011 statistics. As in previous years, separatists frequently targeted government representatives, including teachers and district and municipal officials as well as military personnel, with bombings, shootings, and kidnappings. Separatists also killed and injured both Buddhist and Muslim civilians from many occupations.

Some government-backed civilian defense volunteers, most of them ethnic Thai Buddhists from villages in the South, continued to receive basic training and weapons from security forces. Human rights organizations expressed concerns about vigilantism against ethnic Malay Muslims by these defense volunteers and other civilians.

Abductions

There were no confirmed reports that individuals disappeared after security officials questioned them in the southern provinces. However, reputable NGOs reported the possible forced disappearances of Nasuelan Pi from a tea shop in Narathiwat Province on January 17 by two men in military uniforms, and of Abdullo Kutha after a June 22 meeting with a member of the 43rd Paramilitary Task Force at Ingkhayut Borihan Military Camp in Pattani Province.

In the cases of Ibbroheng Kahong and Dunhami Marae, who were reported missing in April 2011 after they requested the return of their boat seized by the Border Patrol Police in Yala Province, their families were designated during the year as eligible for 7.5 million baht ($245,000) each in compensation from a government program (see section 1.a.). Payment did not occur by year's end.

Physical Abuse, Punishment, and Torture

The government continued to arrest suspected militants, some of them juveniles, and in some cases held them for a month or more under Emergency Decree and martial law provisions. Human rights organizations maintained that the arrests were arbitrary, excessive, and needlessly lengthy, and continued to criticize detention facility overcrowding. Civil society groups accused the army of torturing some suspected militants at detention facilities.

Martial law allows for detention up to seven days, without charge or court or government agency approval in Pattani, Narathiwat, and Yala provinces.

For example, on September 20, authorities arrested Thammarat Alilatae in Yala Province under martial law provisions and detained him for five days without charge before releasing him. (The NGO Group of Fellow Defendants that he founded in 2007 advocates for persons arrested under the special laws in effect in the southernmost provinces.) The Emergency Decree in effect in the same areas allows authorities to arrest and detain suspects for up to 30 days without charge. After the expiration of this period, authorities may begin holding suspects under normal criminal law (see section 1.d.). Unlike under martial law, these latter detentions require court consent, although human rights NGOs complained that courts did not always exercise their right of review. In some cases a suspect was held first under martial law for seven days and then detained for an additional 30 days under the decree. The Southern Border Province Police Command stated that it arrested 109 persons under the decree during the year. The ISOC reported 476 arrests during the year under martial law in the southern provinces of Yala, Pattani, and Narathiwat.

Child Soldiers

Regulations prohibit formal recruitment of children under age 18 to serve as Territorial Defense Volunteers, and in practice volunteers generally joined at age 20 or older, but there continued to be anecdotal information that a small number of children were involved informally in such groups. There were no reports of youth under age 18 conscripted or recruited into governmental armed forces. There were, however, reports of separatist groups recruiting children under age 18 to commit acts of arson or serve as scouts.

The UN Committee on the Rights of the Child issued a report on February 21 that criticized the government's data collection on this problem, including among refugee children. The report also called for further action to prevent the informal involvement of children in village defense militia, criminalize recruitment under age 18, and review military school training that involved children ages 16 to 18.

Also see the Department of State's *Trafficking in Persons Report* at www.state.gov/j/tip.

Other Conflict-Related Abuses

Human rights organizations alleged that the military continued to mail official letters to village headmen or local district officers in the four southernmost provinces, inviting them to nominate a specified number of "voluntary villagers" to attend a workshop. Credible sources claimed that villagers who attended these training sessions had their privacy invaded since they were interrogated and forced to furnish biometric data (fingerprints, DNA samples, and photographs), but this practice has reportedly become less common. Nonetheless, the 2012 ISOC Region 4 Annual Report stated that 73 of the 729 individuals "invited" or "welcomed" to such sessions were also named in arrest warrants. NGOs also reported in December that DNA sampling was required of over 100 men and boys rounded up during recent police raids on three villages in Sai Thong subdistrict, Pattani Province, and at several road checkpoints in the southernmost provinces.

Insurgents burned seven schools in the southernmost provinces during the year, for a total of more than 300 since 2004. The government frequently armed ethnic Thai Buddhist and ethnic Malay Muslim civilians, fortified schools and temples, and provided military escorts to monks and teachers. In some cases the military has used schools as barracks. According to the Ministry of Education, separatist violence killed 202 teachers, students, and education staff and injured 343 others since 2004. The figures for the year were 12 students injured and three killed and two school personnel killed and two injured-- all decreases compared with 2011. Separatist violence also included attacks on medical facilities. According to the NGO Deep South Watch, separatists killed one public health official, the same as in 2011.

Southern insurgents conducted leaflet campaigns during the year, alleging that large numbers of Thai Buddhists have fled violence-affected areas in the South. Although official statistics were not available, there were reports--such as the November 2011 report of the NGO Internal Displacement Monitoring Center--that more than 30 percent of Thai Buddhists and 10 percent of ethnic Malay Muslims have fled such southern areas to other provinces since 2004 (see section 2.d.). Official registration statistics from the Department of Provincial Administration showed that as of December, Yala Province experienced a slight decline in population, but Pattani and Narathiwat provinces had slight increases. Likewise, during the 12-month period ending in September, registration data showed only Yala Province had significantly fewer Buddhists move into (824) rather than out of (4,351) the province; Pattani and Narathiwat provinces' arrival and departure statistics for Buddhist residents were nearly equal. However, official registration data may not accurately reflect numbers of actual residents who may live elsewhere for employment or other reasons. On September 25, the ISOC deputy spokesperson reported more than 125,000 Thai Buddhists living in the three provinces.

SECTION 2. RESPECT FOR CIVIL LIBERTIES, INCLUDING

a. Freedom of Speech and Press

The constitution and law specifically provide for freedom of speech and press with some exceptions, although the government used Emergency Decree authority to limit these rights during the year in southern provinces. The government continued to monitor television and radio broadcasters and exert pressure on broadcast media to cooperate in disseminating constructive and "balanced" news. Nevertheless, the media and civil society vocally criticized government authorities throughout the year. Print, broadcast, and online media covered news critical of the government and its senior-level officials and carried interviews with opposition figures.

The international and independent media operated freely, except in coverage of matters deemed a threat to national security or offensive to the monarchy. By law the government may restrict freedom of expression to preserve national security, maintain public order, preserve the rights of others, protect public morals, and prevent insults to Buddhism. The law also allows police with a court order to restrict or confiscate publications and other materials for disturbing the peace, interfering with public safety, or offending public morals.

In October 2011 the UN special rapporteur on the promotion and protection of the right to freedom of opinion and expression reportedly urged the government to hold public consultations on amending provisions of lese-majeste and computer crime laws in view of their limitations on human rights, their vagueness, and the severity of their penalties. On January 10-16, the rapporteur conducted a series of private consultations, reportedly including meetings with members of both houses of the National Assembly and the NHRC. As of the rapporteur's June 4 report to the UN Human Rights Council, an official visit request was pending.

Freedom of Speech

Criminal Code Article 112, the so-called lese-majeste law, makes it a crime--punishable by up to 15 years' imprisonment for each offense--to criticize, insult, or threaten the king, queen, royal heir apparent, or regent. The law also allows citizens to initiate lese-majeste complaints against each other, and there were several cases in which private citizens did so during the year. Trials may be conducted in secret, and public disclosure of the content of the alleged offenses may be prohibited; international and domestic human rights organizations and academics expressed concern over the chilling effect these factors may have on freedom of expression.

Significantly increased prosecutions for lese-majeste offenses started in 2006 and continued through the year. Official statistics varied by agency, but in the decade before 2006, there were approximately five new lese-majeste charges on average annually, compared with 478 new charges involving Article 112 in 2010, 86 in 2011, and 84 in 2012 that the Office of the Judiciary reported. The overall conviction rate remained nearly 100 percent, and sources estimated that seven to 18 persons remained detained under lese-majeste laws at year's end.

In the case of publisher and labor organizer Somyot Phruksakasemsuk, who remained in custody since his arrest in April 2011 on lese-majeste charges based on two articles published in *Voice of Taksin* magazine in 2010, a trial began in November 2011 and continued at year's end. On October 10, the Constitutional Court rejected Somyot's petition to invalidate Article 112 as unconstitutional and ruled that criminal penalties for lese-majeste offenses were constitutional because such offenses represent threats to national security. The lese-majeste trial of Ekachai Hongkangwan, arrested in 2011 for selling allegedly defamatory videos, began on July 17 and continued at year's end.

During the year there were also notable developments in earlier lese-majeste cases. For example, the criminal court acquitted Sondhi Limthongkul, a People's Alliance for Democracy leader, in September on a 2008 lese-majeste charge, and acquitted Surapak Phuchaisaeng of a 2011 charge and released him in October. On April 19, authorities granted Nat Sattayapornpisut an early release after he served 28 months of a nine-year sentence for a 2009 lese-majeste conviction. Also in April the public prosecutor dropped lese-majeste charges filed in 2008 against Chotisak Onsoong.

Freedom of Press

Government entities owned and controlled all radio and broadcast television stations, including the 524 officially registered "regular" AM and FM stations. The armed forces and police owned another 244 radio stations, ostensibly for national security purposes. Other owners of national broadcast media included the government's Public Relations Department and the Mass Communication Organization of Thailand Public Company Limited, a former state enterprise in which the government maintained a majority share. Nearly all stations are leased to commercial companies that provide commercial content to the stations.

The law provides for the regulation of radio and television frequencies and three categories of broadcast licenses (public service, community service, and commercial). The National Broadcasting and Telecommunications Commission (NBTC) allocates broadcast frequencies and regulates broadcast media. Radio stations must renew their licenses every seven years. Radio signals are broadcast via government transmitters. Stations are required by law to broadcast 30-minute, government-produced newscasts twice daily and to register with the NBTC. Several thousand small community radio stations nationwide also operate under a separate licensing system.

Violence and Harassment

Unlike previous years, there were no reports that journalists were arrested, imprisoned, physically attacked, harassed, or intimidated due to their reporting.

The trial continued at year's end of Batdon Phansaen who was arrested in June 2011 for the killing that month of Sawai Chimphli, a public school teacher and owner of a community radio station in Ubon Ratchathani Province, while he was on the air.

The 2010 killings of two foreign journalists, who died while covering antigovernment protests in Bangkok, remained under investigation by the Department of Special Investigations (see section 1.a.).

On appeal, the Nakhon Pathom Provincial Court in August 2011 reduced to 50 years' imprisonment the death sentences imposed on gunmen Apirak Timpitak and Kamphon Misin but maintained the death sentence imposed on Chanin Leepaiboon, who ordered the 2010 killing of newspaper owner and reporter Kongpop Sawasdi.

Censorship or Content Restrictions

By invoking the Emergency Decree in the three southernmost provinces, the government may restrict print and broadcast media, online news, and social media networks there. The decree empowers the government "to prohibit publication and distribution of news and information that may cause the people to panic or with an intention to distort information." It also authorizes the government to censor news considered a threat to national security.

Journalists generally were free to comment on government activities and institutions without fear of official reprisal. Nonetheless, they occasionally practiced self-censorship, particularly with regard to the monarchy and national security. For example, in April the Thai distributor of *The Economist* magazine withheld one issue because of a story about lese-majeste prosecutions. A journalism institute reported that although the government did not engage in any direct intimidation of print media, it did do so indirectly through its advertising choices.

Broadcast media were subject to government censorship, both directly and indirectly, and self-censorship was also evident. Nevertheless, broadcast media reported criticism of the government.

Libel Laws/National Security

Defamation is a criminal offense, punishable by a fine of up to 200,000 baht ($6,500) and two years' imprisonment. During the year criminal courts made several rulings on defamation and libel cases against political activists and politicians.

On September 27, the criminal court in Bangkok sentenced UDD co-leader Jatuporn Prompan to a suspended term of six months and a fine of 50,000 baht ($1,600) for defaming Democrat Party Leader Abhisit Vejjajiva by stating that he ordered soldiers to kill red-shirt protesters when he was prime minister.

At year's end a further appeal continued in the case of Sondhi Limthongkul, a People's Alliance for Democracy leader, after an appeals court upheld his 2009 defamation conviction but reduced his sentence for statements criticizing a former deputy prime minister during a 2007 television program. He remained free on bail at year's end.

Internet Freedom

The government imposed some restrictions on access to the Internet and reportedly monitored Internet chat rooms and social media without judicial oversight. Individuals and groups generally engaged in the peaceful expression of views via the Internet, including by e-mail, although there were several limitations on content, such as lese majeste, pornography, and gambling. Internet access was widely available and used by citizens, including a government program introduced during the year to provide limited free WiFi access at 200,000 hotspots in cities and schools.

The law establishes procedures for the search and seizure of computers and computer data in certain criminal investigations and gives the Ministry of Information and Communications Technology authority to request and enforce the suspension of information disseminated via computer. A maximum five-year prison sentence and a 100,000 baht ($3,300) fine may be imposed for posting false content on the Internet that undermines public security, causes public panic, or hurts others. A maximum 20-year sentence and 300,000 baht ($9,800) fine may be imposed if an offense results in the death of an individual. The law also obliges Internet service providers to preserve all user records for 90 days in case officials wish to access them. Any service provider who gives consent to or intentionally supports the publishing of illegal content is also liable to punishment. Most prosecutions continued to be for content-related offenses. By law a court order is required to ban a Web site, although this requirement was not always applied in practice. Media activists criticized the law, stating that the offenses were defined too broadly and some penalties were too harsh.

There was continued Internet censorship, and use of the law continued to stifle certain areas of freedom of expression. The government closely monitored and blocked thousands of Web sites that criticized the monarchy. Many political Web boards and discussion forums chose to self-censor and monitor discussions closely to avoid being blocked, and newspapers disabled or restricted access to their public comment sections to minimize exposure to possible lese-majeste charges.

The RTP Electronic Crime Suppression Division reported receiving 776 computer-related complaints during 2011 that resulted in 442 investigations--a complaint rate markedly greater than the 47 in 2009 or 285 in 2010. Most cases involved alleged defamation, lese majeste, and illegal activity such as gambling and pornography. Separately, the Ministry of Information and Communications Technology operated the Cyber Security Operations Center to monitor and block Web sites. According to a report by the NGO iLaw, court orders officially blocked nearly 21,000 Uniform Resource Locators (URLs) during the year, 80 percent of which were related to lese majeste. Since passage of the 2007 Computer Crime Act, authorities blocked more than 102,000 URLs, 76 percent related to lese majeste.

On October 31, the criminal court acquitted and released Surapak Phuchaisaeng, a freelance computer programmer from Nongkhai Province whom authorities arrested in September 2011 and detained without bail for nearly 14 months on the charge of creating an antimonarchy Facebook page.

In May Thanthawut Thaweewarodomkul (also known by his online name, Red Eagle) withdrew his appeal in favor of seeking a royal pardon. Authorities had arrested him in 2010 and sentenced him in March 2011 to 13 years' imprisonment for his role as webmaster of a UDD Web site. (See also section 1.c. regarding the death in May of Amphon Tangnopphakhun, imprisoned for lese-majeste offenses.)

On May 30, a court found Chiranuch Premchaiporn guilty under the Computer Crime Act in the first of two lese-majeste prosecutions against her as executive director of *Prachatai*, an independent online newspaper. In this first high-profile case of intermediary liability under the 2007 law, she was convicted because unrelated third parties posted comments on Prachatai.com that authorities deemed offensive to the monarchy, and she did not remove the comments quickly enough. She received a one-year prison sentence, reduced to eight months and suspended, and a fine of 20,000 baht ($650). During the year *Prachatai* continued its 2010 closure of its public comment Web board to avoid liability under the law.

Academic Freedom and Cultural Events

The government also continued to restrict academic discussions of the monarchy. For example, on January 30, Thammasat University banned a group of its academics, known as "the Nitirat group," from on-campus activities in support of amending the lese-majeste law. The ban was lifted two weeks later. Thammasat University professor and noted historian Somsak Jiamthirasakul, who voluntarily appeared at a police station in May 2011 to be charged with lese majeste for discussing the future of the monarchy, was told to report to the Office of the Attorney General on November 20 but was granted a postponement. His case, based on a complaint an RTA officer filed, remained pending at year's end.

Cultural events may be censored, usually for reasons of public decency. By law the state is also authorized to ban the release of movies that "offend the monarchy, threaten national security, hamper national unity, insult faiths, disrespect honorable figures, challenge morals, or contain explicit sex scenes." The law stipulates that the Film and Video Classification Committee must screen and approve all films to be shown, rented, exchanged, or sold in the country. For example, in April the Thai Film Censorship Board, under the Department of Cultural Promotion of the Ministry of Culture, banned *Shakespeare Must Die*, a film adaptation of William Shakespeare's *Macbeth*, since the film allegedly would cause "divisiveness." The filmmakers' appeals to the NHRC, Administrative Court, and Senate human rights committee were pending at year's end. Additionally, theater owners and broadcasters frequently removed content before submitting films to the board.

b. Freedom of Peaceful Assembly and Association

There were no developments related to the visit requested by the UN special rapporteur on the rights to peaceful assembly and association in September 2011.

Freedom of Assembly

The constitution provides for freedom of assembly, and the government respected this right with some exceptions. Martial law, which gives the military authority to restrict freedom of assembly, remained in effect in 31 border region and southern provinces. The Emergency Decree, in effect in three of the southernmost provinces, also provides authority to limit freedom of assembly.

Surat Thani, Phuket, and Phang Nga provinces have their own regulations that prohibit migrant workers--specifically individuals from Cambodia, Burma, and Laos--from forming gatherings, while Samut Sakhon Province prohibits gatherings of more than five persons. These provisions continued not to be enforced strictly, and there often was no such requirement if the gathering was on private property. Employers and NGOs may request permission from authorities for migrant workers to hold cultural gatherings.

Authorities did not restrict the UDD, which organized the 2010 political protests, from holding gatherings or protests throughout the year, although the Department of Special Investigations, Truth for Reconciliation Commission (see section 5), RTP, NHRC, and RTA continued to investigate those events. These investigations focused on the deaths of UDD demonstrators during the government's response as well as terrorism, lese-majeste, arson, robbery, and other charges against UDD members and demonstrators. At year's end approximately 200 UDD supporters remained in prison for political-protest-related criminal convictions, according to UDD sources.

On December 27, prosecutors filed charges against several leaders of the People's Alliance for Democracy (Sondhi Limthongkul, Chamlong Srimuang, Somkiat Pongpaiboon, Pibhop Dhongchai, Maleerat Kaewka, and Prapan Kunmee) for 2008 protest-related offenses, such as trespassing and blockading government buildings. There were no developments in the cases by year's end.

Freedom of Association

The constitution specifically provides for freedom of association, although exceptions are permitted and were made "to protect public interests, to maintain public peace and order or good morals, or to prevent economic monopoly."

The law prohibits the registration of a political party with the same name or emblem as that of a legally dissolved party.

c. Freedom of Religion

See the Department of State's *International Religious Freedom Report* at www.state.gov/j/drl/irf/rpt.

d. Freedom of Movement, Internally Displaced Persons, Protection of Refugees, and Stateless Persons

The constitution provides for freedom of movement within the country, foreign travel, emigration, and repatriation. The government generally respected these rights in practice, with some exceptions for "maintaining the security of the state, public peace and order or public welfare, town and country planning, or youth welfare."

The government usually cooperated with the Office of the UNHCR and humanitarian organizations in providing protection and assistance to internally displaced persons, refugees, returning refugees, asylum seekers, stateless persons, and other persons of concern, although with restrictions. Cooperation with the UNHCR to protect certain groups remained uneven, which limited the UNHCR's ability to provide its protection to all nationalities.

Authorities continued to treat Burmese refugees and asylum seekers outside of designated border camps as illegal migrants, subject to arrest and detention. The process of bail for detained refugees and asylum seekers, which the government regularized in May 2011, continued to result in the release of limited numbers of detainees. As of September when the bail procedure was suspended for an indefinite period, 12 asylum seekers and 87 refugees were released and not rearrested.

In-Country Movement

The government continued to restrict the free movement of members of hill tribes and other minority groups who were not citizens but held government-issued identity cards. The holders of such cards are prohibited from traveling outside their home districts without prior permission from the district office or outside their home provinces without permission from the provincial governor. Offenders are subject to fines or a jail term of 45 to 60 days. Persons without cards may not travel at all. Human rights organizations reported that police at inland checkpoints often asked for bribes in exchange for allowing stateless persons to move from one district to another.

Refugees residing in the nine refugee camps on the border with Burma were not allowed freedom of movement and were by law confined to the camps, although a few registered refugees were granted permission to travel from one camp to another. A refugee apprehended outside the official camps is subject to a fine, detention, deregistration, and deportation.

Refugees and asylum seekers may not undergo the official migrant worker nationality verification process. Migrant workers who have undergone nationality verification and have passports were free to travel throughout the country. Authorities restricted those holding only work permits from traveling outside the province where they work without official permission.

Authorities required other long-time noncitizen residents, including thousands of ethnic Shan and other non-hill tribe minorities, to seek permission for domestic travel.

Foreign Travel

Other long-time noncitizen residents, including thousands of ethnic Shan and other non-hill tribe minorities, are also required to seek permission from local authorities for foreign travel.

Internally Displaced Persons (IDPs)

Localized annual flooding in some provinces occurred in September and December but did not lead to a repeat of the unprecedented, disastrous flooding in late 2011 that caused the closures of thousands of businesses and displacement of approximately 650,000 workers in 19 provinces. The government established shelters as needed in temples, universities, and stadiums for flood-affected victims countrywide and provided accommodation, food, and medical services. By year's end most 2011-flood-related displaced persons had returned home or received necessary assistance.

Protection of Refugees

Thailand is not a signatory to the 1951 Convention relating to the Status of Refugees or its 1967 Protocol. The NGO Human Rights Watch (HRW) report on September 13 labeled treatment of refugees and asylum seekers as "ad hoc and inadequate." Nevertheless, authorities continued to host significant numbers of refugees, provided some protection against their expulsion or return, and allowed persons fleeing fighting in neighboring countries to cross the border and remain until fighting ceased. In addition, non-Burmese refugees recognized by the UNHCR and registered Burmese refugees residing in official refugee camps were permitted to resettle in third countries.

Access to Asylum

The law does not provide for the granting of asylum or refugee status. Asylum seekers and non-Burmese refugees who reside outside official refugee camps are by law considered illegal migrants. If arrested, they are subject to indefinite detention at IDCs in Bangkok and other provinces.

The results of the pilot screening of Burmese asylum seekers by government-instituted Provincial Admissions Boards (PABs) remained under review by the government, and expansion of the screening process to the remaining five camps did not occur by year's end. An estimated 60,000 Burmese have not registered due to the operationally defunct status of the general PABs.

The UNHCR remained limited in its ability to provide its protection mandate to some Lao Hmong and Burmese outside the official camps as well as to all North Koreans. It continued to have access to asylum seekers in the main IDC in Bangkok and at Suvarnabhumi International Airport to conduct status interviews and monitor new arrivals, but during the year it did not have access to IDCs in coastal Ranong Province to conduct refugee status determinations. Authorities allowed resettlement countries to conduct processing activities in the IDCs, and NGOs were able to provide health care, nutritional support, and other humanitarian assistance.

The government continued to allow the UNHCR to monitor the protection situation of the more than 143,000 Burmese refugees and asylum seekers living in the nine camps along the border with Burma but prohibited the UN agency from having an assistance role in the camps. NGOs, funded by the international community, provided basic humanitarian assistance in the camps, including food, education, shelter, water, sanitation, housing, and other services. Government authorities issued identification cards to registered refugees living in the camps.

Outside the camps, government officials did not distinguish between asylum-seeking Burmese and other undocumented Burmese migrants, regarding all as illegal migrants. Authorities generally took those arrested to the border and deported them.

During the year the government facilitated the resettlement of 7,215 Burmese from camps to other countries. Refugees residing in the nine camps along the border who were not registered with the government were not eligible for third-country resettlement. When registered refugees resettle, unregistered family members were left behind without reunification prospects. In addition, beneficiaries of foreign-government-approved refugee and asylee family-reunification visas were not permitted to depart Thailand, although limited progress was made toward reversing that outcome as these cases were submitted to a newly initiated Fast Track PAB screening process beginning in November. The initial list of 925 family-member reunification cases was submitted to the Fast Track PAB, and the UNHCR continued work on a second list at year's end.

Refoulement

The government provided some protection against the expulsion or return of refugees to countries where their lives or freedom would be threatened on account of their race, religion, nationality, membership in a particular social group, or political opinion, and during the year thousands of asylum seekers entered the country and its refugee camps. However, NGOs estimated that army border units returned thousands of Burmese asylum seekers--mostly those seeking refuge from border skirmishes--to Burma before they could reach established refugee camps. The Mae Sot District IDC in Tak Province deported 170,811 migrants during the year, and the Ranong Province IDC deported 6,694 migrants; some of them might have had asylum claims.

Of the approximately 6,000 Burmese in Thailand in 2011 who had fled fighting between ethnic armies and the Burmese army, at the end of 2012 none reportedly remained at the designated sites outside the official camps where authorities had permitted them to stay.

Immigration Police continued to arrest and detain asylum seekers and refugees in Bangkok, including women and children. Twenty-six refugees and 15 asylum seekers, primarily from Sri Lanka and Vietnam, were known to be in detention in Bangkok at year's end. Upon receipt of bail facilitated by Thai NGOs, authorities released 87 refugees and 12 asylum seekers as of year's end.

Refugee Abuse

Unconfirmed NGO reports in April stated that two Burmese migrants died of suffocation in a truck during a deportation by authorities.

The September 13 HRW report noted that refugees apprehended outside camps were regularly subjected to forced labor and that requests by security forces for unpaid voluntary work in the forest a few times a month were actually mandatory. Refugees also told HRW of physical abuse by Thai camp guards.

Employment

The law prohibits refugees from working in the country. The government allowed undocumented migrant workers from neighboring Burma, Cambodia, and Laos to work legally in certain economic sectors if they registered with authorities and began a process to document their status (see section 7.d.).

Access to Basic Services

The international community provided basic services for refugees living inside closed camps. A complicated medical referral system continued to hamper the ability of refugees to seek some necessary medical services.

Since refugee children generally did not have access to the Thai education system, NGOs continued to provide schooling, with some coordination with the Ministry of Education regarding curriculum.

Temporary Protection

Throughout the year small groups of individuals fleeing fighting in Shan State, Burma, continued to cross into Thailand. There were no reports of their forced return to Burma by the government, although persons of Shan ethnicity were not permitted to enter the refugee camps, pursue refugee status, or seek resettlement to third countries.

Stateless Persons

In the previous four years, the government proceeded to identify stateless individuals, provide documentation to preclude statelessness, and open paths to Thai citizenship for long-time residents. According to the UNHCR, an estimated 500,000 persons, mainly residing in the northern region, could be considered stateless, and several NGOs stated that most may be eligible for citizenship. Many were members of hill tribes, also known as highlanders (see section 6, Indigenous People). Others were migrants from Burma who did not have evidence of Burmese citizenship, ethnic minorities registered with civil authorities, previously undocumented minorities, and displaced persons residing in border camps.

Birth within the country does not automatically confer citizenship. By law citizenship is based on birth to one or both Thai parents, marriage to a Thai man, or naturalization. It may also be acquired by means of special government-designated criteria implemented by the Interior Ministry with approval from the cabinet or as a result of nationality law (see also section 6, Children).

Amendments to the law during the year allow ethnic Thai stateless persons who meet the added definition of "displaced Thai" and their children to apply for the status of "Thai nationality by birth," but there were reports of slow, inconsistent implementation due to labyrinthine laws and regulations and the existence of substantial gray areas within and among them.

The law stipulates that every child born in the country will receive an official birth certificate, regardless of the parents' legal status. Many parents did not obtain birth certificates for their children due to the complexity of the process, the need to travel from remote areas to district offices, and a lack of recognition of the importance of the document. There continued to be reports of some local officials charging for the certificate although it is supposed to be free. During the year authorities issued 3,793 birth certificates in refugee camps, a substantial increase compared with 1,977 in 2011. In some camps birth certificates were issued only to children of registered refugees, but NGO sources noted government progress toward issuance of a certificate to every newborn.

By law, as noncitizens, stateless highlanders may not vote or own land, and their travel is restricted. Stateless persons also may not participate in certain occupations reserved for citizens, including farming, although in practice officials permitted noncitizen highlanders to undertake subsistence agriculture. Stateless persons had difficulty accessing credit and government services, such as education or health care. Many stateless highlanders lived in poverty. Without legal status, stateless persons were vulnerable to various forms of abuse (see also section 6, Children).

SECTION 3. RESPECT FOR POLITICAL RIGHTS: THE RIGHT OF CITIZENS TO CHANGE THEIR GOVERNMENT

The constitution provides citizens the right to change their government peacefully through periodic, free, and fair elections based on universal, compulsory suffrage. The constitution provides for the election of all members of the 500-seat House of Representatives and 77 members of the 150-seat Senate. It also provides for the appointment of 73 additional Senate members by a selection committee composed of members of the judiciary and other regulatory bodies, last designated in April 2011.

Elections and Political Participation

Recent Elections

The July 2011 national election for the House of Representatives generally was considered free and fair, although there were allegations of vote buying, minor procedural irregularities, and scattered but unconfirmed reports of intimidation by local military and government officials. The Election Commission of Thailand (ECT) reported 604 complaints of fraud in 2011-12 in relation to the national election. Among them, the ECT completed 355 investigations--which led to 334 dismissals, 10 reelections, two recounts, and nine findings of fraud that were referred to the Supreme Court--and 249 complaints were dismissed by the ECT or withdrawn by petitioners without full investigation.

In the case of the March 2011 bombing in Prachinburi Province that injured Anon Charoensuk, a local politician and canvasser for the Social Action Party, there were no reported developments by year's end. In the May 2011 shooting of Pracha Prasopdi, a former Puea Thai member of parliament from Samut Prakan Province, the trial of the four accused continued at year's end.

Participation of Women and Minorities

The constitution encourages political parties to consider a "close proximity of equal numbers" of both genders. Women have the right to vote and run for positions, but voters elected relatively few female officials. Besides the country's first female prime minister, Yingluck Shinawatra, the July 2011 national election resulted in 81 women in the 500-seat lower house joining 25 women (12 elected, 13 appointed) in the 150-seat Senate. Women held two of the 36 cabinet positions and chaired two House committees and five of the Senate's 22 standing committees.

Few members of ethnic minorities held positions of authority in national politics. Muslims from the South held significant elected positions at the national level, although they continued to be underrepresented in appointed local and provincial government positions staffed by the centralized national civil service. There were 25 Muslim and eight Christian members of parliament.

SECTION 4. CORRUPTION AND LACK OF TRANSPARENCY IN GOVERNMENT

The law provides criminal penalties for official corruption. Government implementation of the law was weak, and officials sometimes engaged in corrupt practices with impunity.

Corruption remained widespread among members of the police. There were numerous incidents of police charged with abduction, sexual harassment, theft, and malfeasance plus reports that police tortured, beat, and otherwise abused detainees and prisoners, generally with impunity. During the year authorities arrested police officers and convicted them of murder, drug trafficking, and smuggling; police reportedly also were involved with intellectual property rights violations. On August 23, authorities charged two police officers in Bueng Kan Province with running an illegal log-smuggling operation.

The NCCC sent several high-profile cases of malfeasance by officials and politicians to the OAG for prosecution during the year and reported that there were 9,166 cases pending investigation in December. In the 12-month period ending October 1, the NCCC received 2,288 cases and completed 3,642 cases, 212 of which required further action, including disciplinary actions, impeachments, and referrals to the courts, the OAG, or a joint NCCC-OAG committee, and forwarded 2,064 cases to other agencies for investigation.

The OAG prosecution of the case against the former director of the Tourism Authority, Chuthamat Siriwan, and her daughter, Chittisopha Siriwan, for corruption connected to 2010 film festival bribery (found by the NCCC in August 2011), continued at year's end before the Supreme Court of Justice for Persons Holding Political Positions.

At year's end the 2009 warrant for the arrest of former prime minister Thaksin Shinawatra continued in force, and the Supreme Court of Justice's case against him regarding a 2006 government bank loan to Burma remained suspended. He continued to reside outside the country. The NCCC and OAG continued to investigate allegations of corruption committed by members of the government led by prime minster Thaksin from 2001-06, and their findings triggered several cases at the Criminal Division of the Supreme Court of Justice for Persons Holding Political Positions. The court issued an arrest warrant for Thaksin on October 11 in a separate case alleging abuse of power during his premiership in connection with real estate loans issued by a state-run bank. At year's end the trial of seven prominent former government ministers and other high-ranking officials, including former Bangkok Governor Apirak Kosayodhin, on charges of malfeasance related to a 2004 purchase of fire trucks also continued in the Supreme Court of Justice for Persons Holding Political Positions.

Financial disclosure laws and regulations require elected and appointed public officials to disclose assets and income, according to standardized forms and instructions that also include spouses and unmarried children under age 20. On July 24, the NCCC found that Supoj Saplom, a former permanent secretary of the Ministry of Transportation and a civil servant, possessed unexplained wealth, declared assets falsely, and participated in corrupt activities. The NCCC referred the case to the OAG for prosecution and seizure of approximately 65 million baht ($2.1 million) of his assets.

In addition to the NCCC and OAG, the Anti-Money Laundering Office and the Auditor General also investigate and prosecute corruption cases. Other entities with a role in combating corruption included the Supreme Court of Justice, which hears corruption cases; the Ombudsman's Office and Administrative Courts, which accept and investigate complaints; and the Justice Ministry, which oversees cases and develops anticorruption policy in coordination with the others. All these entities complained of resource limitations leading to backlogs, and some complained of political interference. NGOs broadly credited the Ombudsman's Office and NCCC for effective collaboration with civil society. The constitution and law provide public access to government information, and the government effectively implemented the law.

Section 5. Governmental Attitude Regarding International and Nongovernmental Investigation of Alleged Violations of Human Rights

A wide variety of domestic and international human rights organizations generally operated without government restriction, investigating and publishing their findings on human rights cases. However, NGOs that dealt with sensitive political matters, such as opposition to government-sponsored development projects or border matters, continued to face periodic harassment. Human rights workers focusing on violence in the southern provinces were particularly vulnerable to harassment and intimidation by government agents and militant groups. The government accorded very few NGOs tax-exempt status, which sometimes hampered their ability to secure adequate funding.

On November 19, assailant(s) shot and killed Montha Chukaew and Pranee Boonrat, activists in a land dispute involving a palm oil company in Klong Sai, Surat Thani Province. An investigation continued at year's end.

At year's end the trial continued of six persons--Niphon Yantalapha, Chakkraphong Khwanphan-ngam, Yothin Theprien, Sitthichok Nopnom, Thanayot Wongphim, and Phairot Saengsawang--charged with the July 2011 killing of Thongnak Sawekchinda, an environmental activist in Samut Sakhon Province who had protested the transport and use of coal. A seventh defendant, Sutchadet Thapkrai, was killed on May 3 while free on bail.

At year's end the provincial prosecutor's office continued investigating the September 2011 killing of Thatsakamon Ob-om, a leader of the Karen ethnic minority movement in Kaeng Krachan National Reserve forest and a former parliamentary candidate in Phetchaburi Province.

UN and Other International Bodies

The government agreed to schedule visits by the UN special rapporteurs on water and sanitation in 2013 and on torture and other inhumane treatment in 2014. According to UN reports, there were no developments regarding official visits previously requested by the UN working group on disappearances and by the UN special rapporteurs on the freedoms of expression, assembly, and association, and on the situations of human rights defenders, migrants, and IDPs.

Government Human Rights Bodies

The constitution calls for an independent National Human Rights Commission to protect human rights. Composed of seven members selected by the Senate, it is tasked with producing an annual country report. During the year the commission received 734 petitions and completed 664 investigations, but modest staffing and resources continued to hamper progress. The government responded to NHRC recommendations with an explanation or action approximately half the time and adopted approximately one in five recommendations. Although a draft report on the 2010 political protests was leaked in July 2011 and roundly criticized, and the combined 2010-11 report was scheduled for release in early 2012, no official document was published by year's end. Several civil society leaders continued to rate the NHRC poorly and debated publicly whether the weakness was institutional or simply a result of capacity limitations among commissioners.

The Office of the Ombudsman is an independent agency empowered to consider and investigate complaints lodged by any citizen. Following an investigation, the office may refer a case to a court for further review or provide recommendations for further action to the appropriate agency. The office examined all petitions, but it cannot compel agencies to comply with its recommendations. The office is required to submit annual performance reports to the National Assembly but had not done so by year's end. Its 2012 budget was 184 million baht ($6 million), down from 190 million baht ($6.2 million) in 2011. From October 2011 to September 2012, the office received 2,283 new petitions and resolved 2,227 cases. Credible 2010 surveys concluded that approximately half the public trusted the office.

Two parliamentary committees addressed human rights problems: the House Standing Committee on Legal Affairs, Justice, and Human Rights, and the Senate Standing Committee on Human Rights, Rights and Liberties, and Consumer Protection. Human rights advocates generally continued to believe the committees were well intentioned but lacked the enforcement capability required to be effective. The committees also were described as reactive, difficult to access, and hampered by the political affiliations of their chairs.

In 2010, following the dispersal of that year's antigovernment protests, then prime minister Abhisit Vejjajiva, as part of a proposed national reconciliation plan, formed the independent Truth for Reconciliation Commission of Thailand chaired by Khanit na Nakhorn. The administration of Prime Minster Yingluck Shinawatra continued to support the TRCT to complete its two-year mandate and establish causes, document facts, determine appropriate remedies, and recommend steps to prevent a recurrence of large-scale political protests. On September 17, the TRCT released its final report, which assigned blame among many parties, including the protesters, the government and its security forces, the former administration of prime minister Thaksin Shinawatra, and the military officers who ousted him in the 2006 coup. On October 15, the government nominally accepted the report and formed a ministerial committee to study its findings and recommendations, but it took no official implementing actions by year's end.

SECTION 6. DISCRIMINATION, SOCIETAL ABUSES, AND TRAFFICKING IN PERSONS

The constitution provides for equal treatment without respect to race, gender, religion, disability, language, or social status but does not provide for equal treatment without respect to sexual orientation or gender identity. In practice some discrimination existed, and government enforcement of equal protection statutes continued to be uneven.

Women

Rape and Domestic Violence

Rape is illegal, although the government did not always enforce the law effectively. The law permits authorities to prosecute spousal rape, and prosecutions occurred. The police reported receiving 3,527 rape cases during the year, including two cases in which the victim was killed, and they arrested suspects in 2,089 of these cases, including one that resulted in the victim's death.

The law specifies penalties ranging from four years' to life imprisonment, as well as fines, for rape or forcible sexual assault, depending on the age of the victim, severity of the assault, and physical and mental condition of the victim afterward. The amount of the fine depends on the severity of injury to the victim and generally varies from 8,000 to 40,000 baht ($262 to $1,300). The law also provides that any individual convicted twice for the same type of criminal rape within three years is liable to receive increased penalties for recidivism.

According to court statistics, authorities filed 4,053 cases involving sexual assault with the courts--a marked increase, compared with 2011. The case completion rate and sentencing information were not available.

NGOs believed that rape continued to be a serious problem. Academics and women's rights activists maintained that rapes and domestic assaults were underreported, in part because state agencies tasked with addressing the problem continued to be inadequately funded, and survivors perceived law enforcement agencies to be incapable of bringing perpetrators to justice. Police sought to change this perception and continued to encourage women to report sexual crimes through the use of female police officers in metropolitan Bangkok and three other provinces.

Domestic violence against women continued to be a significant problem. The Health Ministry reported overall that 11,074 women older than age 18 reported abuse in 2011 and sought assistance from the ministry's One Stop Crisis Center. Of these victims, 79 percent reported physical abuse, and 16 percent reported sexual abuse. The law imposes a fine of up to 6,000 baht ($200) or up to six months' imprisonment for violators and provides authorities, with court approval, the power to prohibit offenders from remaining in their homes or contacting family members during trial. The law also establishes measures designed to facilitate both the reporting of domestic violence complaints and reconciliation between the victim and the perpetrator. Additionally, the law restricts media reporting on domestic violence cases in the judicial system.

Authorities prosecuted some domestic violence crimes, particularly cases where the victim was seriously injured, under provisions for assault or violence against a person, where they could seek harsher penalties. Domestic violence frequently went unreported, however, and police often were reluctant to pursue reports of domestic violence. NGO-supported programs included emergency hotlines, temporary shelters, and counseling services to increase awareness of domestic violence, HIV/AIDS, and other matters involving women. The government's crisis centers, located in some state-run hospitals, cared for abused women and children, although several centers faced budget difficulties. State-run hospitals referred abused women to external organizations when in-hospital services were not available.

The Ministry of Social Development and Human Security (MSDHS) reported that it recorded 700 cases of domestic violence nationwide during the year. In 139 cases the victim pursued criminal charges, while in 333 cases the victim chose not to do so. Sixty-nine cases remained in consultation at year's end; the disposition of the remaining cases was unknown. As of October, 50 of the criminal cases were under police or public prosecutors' investigation and court mediation or in trial, and 44 cases were completed. Sentencing information continued to be unavailable.

The MSDHS continued to develop a community-based system, operating in all regions of the country, to protect women from domestic violence. The program focused on training community representatives from each community on women's rights and abuse prevention to increase community awareness.

Sexual Harassment

Sexual harassment is illegal in both the public and private sectors. The law specifies fines of not more than 20,000 baht ($650) for individuals convicted of sexual harassment. The punishment depends on the degree of harassment and age of the victim. Abuse categorized as an indecent act may result in imprisonment of up to 15 years and a fine of up to 30,000 baht ($980). The law governing the civil service also prohibits sexual harassment and stipulates five levels of punishment: probation, docked salary, salary decrease, suspension, and termination. NGOs claimed that the legal definition of harassment was vague and prosecution of harassment claims difficult. Data on the numbers of abusers prosecuted, convicted, and punished were unavailable.

Reproductive Rights

Couples and individuals could decide freely and responsibly the number, spacing, and timing of children, and they had the information and means to do so free from discrimination, coercion, and violence. The publicly funded medical system provided access to contraceptive services and information, prenatal care, skilled attendance during childbirth, and essential obstetric and postpartum care.

According to UN data published in 2011, approximately 80 percent of women and girls ages 15 to 49 used modern contraception methods. Although statistics were unavailable, the percentages of males, ethnic minorities, and migrant workers who had access to contraception were estimated to be lower. Skilled health personnel attended approximately 98 percent of births. Prenatal and postnatal care was estimated to be accessible by more than 90 percent of mothers and babies.

Discrimination

Women generally enjoy the same legal status and rights as men. On July 18, the government withdrew its reservation to article 16 of the Convention on the Elimination of All Forms of Discrimination against Women. Nonetheless, women experienced discrimination on occasion.

The law does not mandate nondiscrimination based on gender in hiring practices, and discrimination in hiring was common. For example, it is not illegal to ask a prospective employee for family status during an interview. Women are not allowed to work in all the same industries as men. Government regulations require employers to pay equal wages and benefits for equal work, regardless of gender. Nonetheless, in practice women continued to receive lower pay for equal work in many sectors of the economy, and women were concentrated in lower-paying jobs. Women were able to own and manage businesses freely.

Women were unable to confer citizenship on their nonnational spouses in the same way as men.

Military academies (except for the nursing academy) continued not to accept female students, although a significant number of instructors were women. According to the Armed Forces Personnel Directorate, 61 women held the rank of general or equivalent across all military branches and within the Ministry of Defense as of December. The Police Cadet Academy for commissioned officers accepts female cadets, and 90 of 240 places in the 2013 cadet class were reserved for women. The first female cadet class was scheduled to graduate from the four-year program in 2013. According to the Office of the Civil Service Commission, women held 26 percent of executive-level civil service positions at year's end.

The government's Bureau of Women's Affairs and Family Development was designed to promote the legal rights of women, notably through the suboffice of the Bureau of Gender Equality Promotion, but it is not an independent agency. It worked with NGOs and did not take a leading role in women's rights.

Children

Birth Registration

Birth within the country does not automatically confer citizenship, but all children born in Thailand are entitled to birth registration (see section 2.d., Stateless Persons, for legal provisions on citizenship). According to NGOs, highlanders and other stateless individuals on occasion did not register births with the authorities, especially births in remote areas, because administrative complexities, misinformed and unscrupulous local officials, language barriers, and restricted mobility continued to make it difficult to do so.

Education

Violence in the southern provinces, especially aimed at public school teachers, sporadically forced the temporary closure of public schools and disrupted the educational process there.

Many NGOs reported that children of registered migrant workers, particularly in Samut Sakhon and Chiang Mai provinces and Mae Sot District, in practice have more limited access to schooling due to frequent relocation to new job sites, distance from school, and their lack of Thai language. These children also remained without access to community services provided to children attending public schools, such as day-care centers, and government-subsidized free milk and lunch. Migrant workers who could afford to pay often chose to send their children to private nurseries or day-care centers at their own expense.

Child Abuse

The law provides for the protection of children from abuse, and laws on rape and abandonment carry harsher penalties if the victim is a child. The law imposes a jail term of seven to 20 years' imprisonment and a fine of up to 40,000 baht ($1,300) for sexual intercourse with a victim under age 13. If the victim is between ages 13 and 15, the penalty is four to 20 years' imprisonment and the same range of fines.

The Health Ministry reported that 11,491 children reported abuse in 2011 and sought assistance from the ministry's One Stop Crisis Center. Of these victims, 74 percent reported sexual abuse, and 21 percent reported physical abuse. Police continued their reluctance to investigate abuse cases, and rules of evidence made prosecution of child abuse difficult. The law is designed to protect witnesses, victims, and offenders under age 18, and procedures--with a judge's consent-- allow children to testify in abuse and pedophilia cases on videotape in private surroundings in the presence of a psychologist, psychiatrist, or social worker. However, many judges declined to use videotaped testimony, citing technical problems and the inability to question accusers and defendants directly in court. Some children's advocates claimed that sexually abused girls received better physical and psychological care than male victims did. Authorities charged persons accused of pedophilia under appropriate age-of-consent and prostitution laws.

Child Marriage

The minimum legal age for marriage for both sexes is 17 years; however, anyone below age 20 requires parental consent. A court may grant permission to marry for those ages 15-16. Awareness programs by Islamic committees and government agencies sought to prevent child marriage under Islamic tradition.

Sexual Exploitation of Children

Child prostitution remained a problem. According to government officials, academics, and NGO representatives, boys and girls, especially among migrant populations, were sometimes coerced or lured into prostitution. While it was widely believed that there were fewer incidents of forced prostitution, children from poor families remained vulnerable, and there continued to be some incidents and arrests of parents who forced their children into prostitution. Citizens and foreign sex tourists continued to commit pedophilia.

The law imposes heavy penalties on whoever procures, lures, compels, or threatens children under age 18 for the purpose of prostitution and provides that a customer who has sexual intercourse with a prostitute under age 15 shall be subject to two to six years in prison and a fine of up to 120,000 baht ($3,900). If the prostitute is between the ages of 15 and 18, the prison term is one to three years, and the fine is up to 60,000 baht ($2,000). Authorities may also punish parents who allow a child to enter into prostitution and revoke their parental rights. Those who procure children for prostitution faced strict penalties, and the punishment was more severe if the minors involved are under age 15. The law prohibits the production, distribution, import, or export of child pornography. The penalty is imprisonment for up to three years and a maximum fine of 6,000 baht ($200). The law also imposes heavy penalties on persons who sexually exploit persons younger than age 18 and defines punishments for pimping, trafficking for labor exploitation, and human smuggling. The government increased enforcement efforts during the year, but some NGOs considered enforcement inadequate.

The UN Committee on the Rights of the Child issued a report on February 17 that criticized the government's data collection on this problem and called for further action. Specific actions included planning comprehensive enforcement measures; coordinating and training government entities and personnel; raising public awareness; strengthening laws, especially on the sale of children and child pornography; preventing child sex tourism; and improving assistance and support to child victims.

Displaced Children

Authorities generally referred street children to government-provided shelters, but many, especially foreign illegal migrants, reportedly avoided the shelters due to fear of deportation. Ultimately the government sent citizen street children to school, occupational training centers, or their families with social-worker supervision. Some street children from other countries were repatriated.

National reports on child labor often omitted street children, and national statistics on street children often included only citizens. While there continued to be no reliable statistics on the numbers of beggars, they included homeless children; kidnapped children; and children who were deployed by parents during school break, evenings after school, or weekends. Some migrants compelled their children to beg to contribute to household income.

International Child Abductions

The country is a party to the 1980 Hague Convention on the Civil Aspects of International Child Abduction. For information see the Department of State's annual compliance report at http://travel.state.gov/abduction/resources /congressreport/congressreport_4308. html, as well as country-specific information at http://travel.state.gov/abduction/country/country 3781.html.

Anti-Semitism

The Jewish community is very small, and there were no reports of anti-Semitic incidents.

Trafficking in Persons

See the Department of State's *Trafficking in Persons Report* at www.state.gov/j/tip.

Persons with Disabilities

The constitution and law prohibit discrimination against persons with physical, sensory, intellectual, and mental disabilities in education, air travel and other transportation, access to health care, or the provision of other state services. Although many public accommodations and buildings were modified to accommodate persons with disabilities, government enforcement was not consistently effective. The law also mandates that persons with disabilities have access to information, communications, and newly constructed buildings, but these provisions were not uniformly enforced. The law allows employment discrimination against persons with disabilities, and activists continued to work for amendments.

Persons with disabilities who register with the government are entitled to free medical examinations, wheelchairs, and crutches. The government provided five-year, interest-free, small business loans for persons with disabilities.

The Community Based Rehabilitation Program remained active in all provinces, while the Community Learning Center for People with Disabilities project operated in 30 provinces and during the year began its expansion to all provinces. A National People with Disabilities Day is observed annually on November 14.

The government maintained 43 special schools for students with disabilities, 76 centers offering special education programs for preschool-age children, and 76 educational centers for persons with disabilities. The law requires all state schools nationwide--approximately 31,000--to accept students with disabilities, and about two-thirds taught such students during the year. There were some reports of schools turning away students with disabilities, although the government claimed that such incidents occurred because schools did not have appropriate facilities to accommodate them. There also were nine government-operated and at least 23 NGO-operated training centers for persons with disabilities, including both full-time and part-time or seasonal centers. The government operated 13 state shelters specifically for persons with disabilities, including two day-care centers for autistic children. In addition, there were private associations providing occasional training for persons with disabilities.

Some employers subjected persons with disabilities to wage discrimination. Government regulations require private firms either to hire one person with a disability for every 100 other workers or contribute to a fund that benefits persons with disabilities, but this provision continued not to be uniformly enforced.

Government officials estimated that 56 percent of firms complied with the law during the year, while the chair of the Council of Disabled People of Thailand believed the number to be 35 to 45 percent, which he attributed primarily to inadequate government follow-up with companies. Some state enterprises had discriminatory hiring policies.

National/Racial/Ethnic Minorities

Two groups--former belligerents in the Chinese civil war and their descendants living in the country since the end of the civil war, and children of Vietnamese immigrants who reside in 13 northeastern provinces--continued to live under laws and regulations that could restrict their movement, residence, education, and occupation. A law confined the Chinese to living in the three northern provinces of Chiang Mai, Chiang Rai, and Mae Hong Son. According to the Interior Ministry, authorities granted approximately 1,000 persons citizenship or legal alien status during the year, thus permitting them to reside elsewhere.

On August 31, the UN Committee on the Elimination of Racial Discrimination issued a report calling for the country to introduce a definition of racial discrimination into its legislation to make it punishable by law and to study the possible discriminatory effects of existing law and policy. The report also highlighted committee concern for ethnic Malay women facing ethnic and religious discrimination in many fields of political and social life.

Indigenous People

Noncitizen members of hill tribes continued to face restrictions on their movement, could not own land, had difficulty accessing bank credit, and although protected by labor laws, often were subjected to labor violations. The law also bars them from state welfare services, such as universal health care. An NGO reported that government medical and education services for some indigenous persons were improving.

The law provides citizenship eligibility to certain categories of highlanders who were not previously eligible (see also section 2.d., Stateless Persons).

Although the government supported efforts to register citizens and educate eligible hill tribe persons about their rights, activists reported that widespread corruption and inefficiency, especially among highland village headmen and district and subdistrict officials, continued to contribute to a persistent backlog of pending citizenship applications as well as improperly denied applications. For example, the NGO International Justice Mission reported in December that an official in Chiang Dao District, Chiang Mai Province, reportedly delayed hundreds of citizenship applications.

Hill tribe members continued to face societal discrimination arising in part from the belief that they were involved in drug trafficking and environmental degradation.

Societal Abuses, Discrimination, and Acts of Violence Based on Sexual Orientation and Gender Identity

No laws criminalize sexual orientation or consensual same-sex sexual conduct between adults.

Lesbian, gay, bisexual, and transgender (LGBT) groups were able to register with the government, although there were some restrictions on the wording used in registering their group names. They reported that police treated LGBT victims of crime the same as other persons except in the case of sexual crimes, where there continued to be a tendency to downplay sexual abuse or not to take harassment seriously.

The law does not permit transgender individuals to change their gender on identification documents. Nonetheless, in August the Interior Ministry allowed an intersex person, Sirilada Khotphat, to change her listed gender from male to female, the first such decision. In addition, on May 27, voters elected Yollada Suanyot to the Nan Provincial Administration as the country's first transgender provincial councilor, sparking public debate about identification policy due to civil service dress code requirements--Yollada has lived as a woman since age 16 but continued to carry her male birth name on her identity card.

In September 2011 Bangkok's Central Administrative Court ordered the Ministry of Defense to stop describing transgender persons as "permanently mentally disabled" in conscription records. The military complied, and personnel records reportedly indicate "current sexual status contrary to sexual status at birth." Some rights advocates considered this a significant step toward reducing the harmful effects on future employment opportunities caused by the terms formerly used in such records.

For the first time, university rectors permitted five transgender students to participate in the August 30 commencement ceremony for Thammasat University's graduating class while wearing gender-specific uniforms of their choice. This decision set a precedent followed by several other educational institutions during the year. Such permissions remained voluntary for each school.

There was some continued commercial discrimination based on sexual orientation and gender identity. For example, some life insurance companies refused to issue policies to gay men, although at least four of 23 companies sold policies to LGBT citizens with provisions for full transfer of benefits to same-sex partners. NGOs alleged that some nightclubs, bars, hotels, and factories denied entry or employment to gay, lesbian, and transgender individuals.

Other Societal Violence or Discrimination

Persons with HIV/AIDS faced the psychological stigma associated with rejection by family, friends, colleagues, teachers, and the community, although continued intensive educational outreach efforts by the government and NGOs may have reduced this stigma in some communities. There were continued reports that some employers refused to hire persons who tested HIV-positive following employer-mandated blood screening. According to the Thailand Business Coalition on AIDS, 1,767 businesses pledged during the year not to require HIV/AIDS tests for employees nor to discharge infected employees and also vowed to hold regular awareness campaigns.

The 2011 NHRC investigation into the case of the so-called AIDS temple, Wat Phrabat Namphu, which sheltered many dying AIDS patients and displayed their corpses as a caution, was closed on September 17 with no further action after the temple voluntarily ended this practice.

Section 7. Worker Rights

a. Freedom of Association and the Right to Collective Bargaining

The law, including related regulations and statutory instruments, allows private sector workers to form and join trade unions of their choosing without prior authorization, but it does not allow civil servants, including public schoolteachers, soldiers, and police, to form or register a union. By law civil servants may form and register associations, but these associations do not have the right to bargain collectively.

State-owned enterprise workers by law have the right to form unions. Noncitizen migrant workers, whether registered or illegally present, do not have that right nor the right to serve as union officials, but registered migrants may be members of unions organized and led by Thai citizens. The law restricts affiliations between state enterprise unions and private sector unions.

The law prohibits antiunion actions by employers, but this protection does not apply until the union is registered. To register a union, at least 10 workers must submit their names to the Department of Labor Protection and Welfare, which verifies the names with the employer, potentially exposing the workers to retaliation before registration is complete. Additionally, the law requires that union officials be full-time employees of the company or state enterprise. The law prohibits permanent union staff, thus limiting the ability of unions to organize in depth and be politically active. Employers may dismiss workers for any reason, provided severance payment is made. The law does not provide for reinstatement, but a court decision may allow for employee reinstatement and compensation of salary for losses while absent from work. For example, three labor leaders, whom Yum Restaurants International (Thailand) fired for organizing a union, returned to work in December 2011 as a result of a Labor Relations Committee (LRC) reinstatement order. However, during the year the company appealed to the Central Labor Court and reportedly transferred the three individuals to different jobs, where they were isolated from coworkers. At least one of the three resigned.

The law permits workers to strike after an employee has submitted a demand resulting in a deadlock between the employer and employee. Workers must submit a letter of notification at least 24 hours in advance. The government has the authority to restrict private sector strikes that would affect national security or cause severe negative repercussions for the population at large, but it seldom invoked this provision and did not do so during the year.

The law forbids strikes in "essential services," which are defined more broadly than they are under International Labor Organization (ILO) criteria and include sectors such as telecommunications and public transportation. The law prohibits the termination of employment of legal strikers, but employers are permitted to hire workers to replace strikers. Strike action in the private sector was constrained by the legal requirement to call a general meeting of trade union members and obtain strike approval by at least 50 percent of all union members.

The law provides for the right of private sector citizen workers to organize and bargain collectively and defines the mechanisms for collective bargaining, government-assisted conciliation, and arbitration in cases under dispute.

Labor law enforcement was inconsistent and in some instances ineffective in protecting workers who participated in union activities. For example, even when labor courts ordered employee reinstatement when dismissal resulted from union activity, the process was lengthy and costly for the employee. Most cases were settled out of court through severance payments to the employee with no effective punishment of the employer.

A system of labor courts exercised judicial review over most aspects of labor law for the private sector. The Ministry of Labor reported that 20,847 charges were referred to the court of first instance, the Central Labor Court, in 2011; most conflicts involved dismissals, violations of law, and working-condition agreements. According to the Supreme Court, approximately 1,100 new labor case appeals were submitted during the year. Due to the backlog of more than 2,166 cases from the previous year, in which only 257 cases were adjudicated, more than 3,000 cases awaited a court decision as of the end of 2011.

Problems of collective labor relations were adjudicated through the tripartite LRC and were subject to labor court review. Workers may also seek redress through the NHRC. In private sector labor disputes that cannot be resolved through negotiation or voluntary arbitration and may affect the national economy or public order, the Ministry of Labor may refer them to the LRC for settlement but seldom used this legal authority. The State Enterprise Relations Committee handled redress of grievances for state enterprise workers. Labor leaders generally were satisfied with the treatment that their concerns received in these forums, although they continued to complain that unjustly dismissed union leaders were awarded only back wages with no punitive sanctions against the employer, thus failing to dissuade employers from illegal actions.

A substantial number of migrants worked in factories near border-crossing points, where there were frequent reports of law violations and few labor inspections. Labor inspectors generally could not speak the languages of migrant workers, which hampered the ability of migrant workers to report violations. During the year the Ministry of Labor reported establishing a center with an interpreter in each of the following 11 provinces with significant migrant-worker populations: Samut Sakhon, Kanchanaburi, Chonburi, Rayong, Chiang Mai, Khon Kaen, Trang, Phuket, Ranong, Songkhla, and Tak. Unionization rates were generally low in industries that employ migrant workers. In a small number of cases, documented migrants did join unions run by Thai nationals, but language barriers and the segregation of Thai and migrant workers by industry limited the impact of these unions on the migrant labor force.

Labor activists and some civil servants interpreted the constitution as broadening the freedom of association to include granting civil servants the right to form a union, and a small number of civil servants attempted to organize a union in 2011, but the law continued to prohibit civil servant unions.

The law constrained the capacity and sustainability of unions by forbidding them from having their own experts or staff members present in negotiations with employers. The law allows only two government-licensed outside advisers to assist a union in collective bargaining. Since unions must use advisers the employer deems acceptable, in practice employers had the freedom to choose their advisers at the collective bargaining table, but labor unions did not. Union leaders and outside observers noted that this interfered with the ability to negotiate, train union members, and develop expertise in collective bargaining and that it contributed to rapid turnover in union leaders.

During 2011 the Department of Labor Protection and Welfare reported 179 informal conflicts between employers and employees involving 103,594 employees: Of these, 138 conflicts were resolved without walkouts, six were referred to a labor court, and 20 continued under the department's process. The department also reported 110 formal labor disputes, a significant increase from 66 in 2010, and eight lockouts with six strikes that involved 1,523 employees. Most disputes were related to wages and other benefits.

Employers continued to discriminate against workers who sought to organize unions. While the law protects workers who submit demands relating to working conditions, it does not protect workers from employer reprisal for union activities prior to a union's registration. There were also cases reported of employers dismissing workers from their jobs for engaging in union activities. In some cases the labor courts ordered workers reinstated if the grounds for their dismissal were proven unlawful. However, there were cases reported of reinstated union workers being transferred to a different job or an inactive position or placed in training, rather than being allowed to continue in their previous position.

Labor activists said the requirement for half of union members to approve labor actions sets a high barrier against conducting a legal strike. Some employers used unfavorable work assignments and reductions in work hours and bonuses to punish strikers. According to the ILO, the law provides penalties, including imprisonment and possible compulsory labor, for strikers in state-owned enterprises.

As of year's end the Supreme Court of Justice continued to consider the appeal by the State Railway Workers Union of Thailand of the July 2011 ruling by the Central Labor Court. The ruling upheld the request of State Railways of Thailand (SRT) to dismiss seven union leaders who had organized a work stoppage to protest unsafe locomotives after a crash in Prachuap Khiri Khan Province in 2009 resulted in seven fatalities. On March 26, the Central

Labor Court dismissed the SRT's 70 million baht ($2.3 million) damage claim against the union leaders, and the SRT's appeal continued at year's end.

Labor brokerage firms use a "contract labor system" under which workers sign an annual contract. Although contract laborers performed the same work as direct-hire workers, employers often paid them less and provided fewer, or no, benefits. By law businesses must provide contract laborers "fair benefits and welfare without discrimination." Regardless of whether the contract labor employee was outsourced and collected wages from a separate company, by law the contracting business is the overall employer, and the law requires equal pay and benefits for subcontract and regular employees. Nonetheless, there were reports during the year of a canned fruit and juice company that made unlawful deductions from migrant worker wages to repay the costs of smuggling, registration, and permits. Workers also reported several other violations by contractors, including failure to pay holiday overtime; provide equipment, uniforms, or adequate drinking water; or pay daily minimum wages for less than eight hours of work. Workers further reported deductions from wages for sick leave absences and bribes to government officials to ignore undocumented workers.

Legal definitions of who may join a union ("employees working for the same employer" or "employees in the same description of work") and requirements that the union represent a certain percentage of the workforce could combine to hamper collective bargaining efforts if contract workers, who made up a substantial portion of the workforce, were not considered part of the potential bargaining unit. Because the law classifies contract workers as working in the "service industry," as opposed to the "manufacturing industry," they may not join an industrial union. This restriction on joining with full-time employees of industries often diminished the ability to bargain collectively as a larger group.

b. Prohibition of Forced or Compulsory Labor

The law prohibits forced or compulsory labor, except in the case of national emergency, war, martial law, or imminent public calamity. Despite efforts by the government to enforce and raise awareness of the law, problems of forced labor of men, women, and children persisted in a small proportion of the economy, particularly in those sectors where foreign migrant labor was common.

Reports of sweatshops and abusive treatment continued in a few sectors, including Thai-flagged seagoing trawlers, garment factories, and shrimp- and seafood-processing facilities. The large numbers of migrants from Burma, Cambodia, and Laos in those sectors created opportunities for abuse (see sections 7.c. and 7.d.). For example, workers reported that employers prevented workers, particularly migrant workers, from changing employers to obtain higher wages when the government decided to increase the daily minimum wage but implement it initially in seven provinces.

During the year there were also reports of employers who kept possession of migrant workers' registration and travel documents, which restricted their movement outside the work site, despite laws prohibiting this practice.

Also see the Department of State's *Trafficking in Persons Report* at www.state.gov/j/tip.

c. Prohibition of Child Labor and Minimum Age for Employment

Legal protections generally exist for children in the formal economic sector. The law regulates the employment of children under age 18 and prohibits employment of children under age 15, although an exception exists for children 13 to 15 years old who have parental permission to perform agricultural work during school breaks or nonschool hours as long as the employers provide a safe work environment.

Employers may not require children under age 18 to work overtime or on a holiday and may not require work between 10 p.m. and 6 a.m. without prior Labor Ministry approval. Children under age 18 must not be employed in hazardous work, which includes any activity involving metalwork, hazardous chemicals, poisonous materials, radiation, and harmful temperatures or noise levels; exposure to toxic microorganisms; operation of heavy equipment; work underground or underwater; and work in places where alcohol is sold or in massage parlors. The maximum penalty for violating these prohibitions is one year in prison, fines up to 200,000 baht ($6,500), or both.

The law provides limited coverage to child workers in some informal sectors, such as fishing and domestic employment, and allows for issuance of ministerial regulations to address sectors not therein covered. Such regulations increased protections for child workers in domestic and agricultural sector work.

The Ministry of Labor's Department of Labor Protection and Welfare is the primary agency charged with enforcing child labor laws and policies. Observers considered labor inspectors to be too few in number and insufficiently responsive to complaints. In an effort to improve enforcement, the ministry's inspection plan for the year continued to prioritize labor inspections of small factories (those with fewer than 50 workers), which were believed to be high risk for the use of child labor. In line with prevailing cultural norms, the inclination of labor inspectors when dealing with violators was to negotiate promises of better future behavior rather than seek prosecution and punishment. The legal requirement for a warrant hampered inspection of private homes to monitor the welfare of child domestic workers.

On November 9, the labor minister approved a new list of hazardous work for child labor that added a clause prohibiting children under age 18 from working on seagoing fishing vessels--a more strict provision than the Labor Protection Act that allows children ages 16-18 to work on fishing vessels. The updated list integrated work and working conditions considered hazardous to the development, health, and welfare of children under age 18 from all other related laws and aimed at raising public awareness and guiding labor inspectors in their inspections of youth labor (ages 15-18).

The Social Security Office under the Labor Ministry reported 66,138 children ages 15-18 formally working and registered in the social security system in 2011, an almost 30 percent increase compared with 2010. The Department of Labor Protection and Welfare reported that labor inspectors inspected 2,106 working children between ages 15 and 17 in 2011 and found no violations. The number of working children inspected in 2011 decreased from 3,624 in 2010 due to the severe flooding in central Thailand that obstructed government operations.

Children (sometimes underage) were found working in agriculture, the garment industry, seafood processing, fishing-related industries, and the informal sector. There was reason to believe that child labor produced and processed some garments, pornography, shrimp, and sugarcane in violation of international standards. In urban areas most underage individuals worked in the service sector, including in gasoline stations, small-scale industries, and restaurants. Observers continued to believe that while the prevalence decreased, some children (usually foreign) were exploited in street selling, begging, commercial sex, domestic service, and agriculture work, sometimes in a system of debt bondage. Many of these foreign children, predominantly migrants from Burma, Cambodia, and Laos, were in the country illegally, which increased their vulnerability to exploitation. There continued to be reports of street children who were bought, rented, or forcibly "borrowed" from their parent(s) or guardian(s) to beg alongside women in the street.

Beyond urban areas, children worked in agriculture, garment, and fishing-related industries. Child labor was less evident but still reportedly present in larger, export-oriented factories and registered processing facilities. Child labor also existed to a lesser degree in export/secondary-processing factories in shrimp- and seafood-processing sectors. NGOs reported some cases of child labor in garment factories along the Burmese border in Mae Sot District.

The total number of child laborers, legal and illegal, continued to be much larger when statistics considered child laborers in the informal sector, including unregistered migrant children. However, there was no comprehensive survey of child labor throughout the country.

Also see the Department of Labor's *Findings on the Worst Forms of Child Labor* at www.dol.gov/ilab/programs/ocft/tda.htm.

d. Acceptable Conditions of Work

The national daily minimum wage increased in April by a countrywide average of 40 percent from a range of 159-221 baht to a range of 222-300 baht (from $5.20- $7.23 to $7.26-$9.81), the largest ever such increase. Minimums continued to vary based on the cost of living in each province. In 2013 the government planned to extend the 300-baht minimum from seven provinces to nationwide. The national poverty line was 54.13 baht/person/day ($1.77).

By law employers are subject to fines up to 100,000 baht ($3,300) and/or imprisonment up to six months for minimum wage noncompliance. After implementation of the new minimum wage, the Labor Solidarity Committee reported receiving complaints from thousands of workers, particularly in hotel, transport, automobile, and jewelry industries, that employers did not raise their wages and cut some benefits, especially in the textile industry. Several worker groups protested in April and May, demanding the minimum wage increase without decreased benefits. A Ministry of Labor survey released in October found that less than 1 percent of workplaces reduced the number of workers, but 6 percent reduced welfare and other benefits. Additionally, labor activists reported an increased number of disputes between employers and skilled workers seeking to increase their daily wages to maintain the gap between unskilled and skilled wages.

The Ministry of Labor is responsible for ensuring that employers adhere to minimum wage requirements in the formal sector, but enforcement was mixed.

Some formal sector workers nationwide received less than the minimum wage, particularly in rural provinces. The ministry reported that more than 99 percent of inspected workplaces (44,224 workplaces) paid the minimum wage. Most noncompliant employers were small enterprises with fewer than 50 workers. Such labor protections also apply to undocumented workers, but many unskilled and semiskilled undocumented migrant workers labored for wages that were at times significantly less than the minimum.

The maximum workweek by law is 48 hours, or eight hours a day over six days, with a limit on overtime of 36 hours per week. Employees engaged in "dangerous" work, such as chemical, mining, or other industries involving heavy machinery, may work a maximum of 42 hours per week and are not permitted overtime. Petrochemical industry employees may not work more than 12 hours per day and may work continuously only for a period not exceeding 28 days. Legal protections do not apply to all sectors. For example, the law does not completely cover household domestic workers.

The ministry also enforces laws related to occupational safety and health. The Occupational Safety, Health, and Environment Act and the Home-based Worker Protection Act that became effective in 2011 impose a maximum sentence of one year's imprisonment and fines not exceeding 400,000 baht ($13,000) on employers for violations. These acts require safe and healthy workplaces and bring home-based businesses into the formal economy. They also prohibit pregnant women and children under age 15 from working in hazardous conditions (as detailed in ministerial regulations).

In 2011 the ministry employed approximately 600 inspectors for an estimated 345,000 workplaces. They inspected 17,039 workplaces employing 1.5 million workers during 2011, according to ministry statistics, and found 1,809 workplaces (more than 10 percent) failed to comply with health and safety regulations, most involving fire accidents; failure to establish safety committees; and inappropriate levels of heat, light, and noise. The ministry also inspected 31,551 informal workers in the home-based business and agriculture sectors. According to the Department of Labor Protection and Welfare, the incidence of violations regarding workers' safety was highest in manufacturing, wholesale and retail trade, construction, hotels, and restaurants. While the majority of violations were resolved after the department issued orders to companies to make amends, there were at least 75 court cases filed.

During 2011 there were 129,632 reported incidents of diseases and injuries from industrial accidents, including 91,699 minor disabilities (resulting in no more than three days' work missed) and 37,933 disabilities resulting in more than three days' work missed (including permanent disabilities and deaths). The rate of incidents occurring in the informal and agricultural sectors and among migrant workers was believed to be higher but underreported. Occupational diseases rarely were diagnosed or compensated, and few doctors or clinics specialized in them. Many young migrant women employed along the border with Burma had limited, substandard medical-care options. Medium- and large-sized factories often applied government health and safety standards, but overall enforcement of safety standards continued to be lax. In the informal sector, health and safety protections continued to be substandard.

Redress for workers injured in industrial accidents continued usually to be untimely and insufficient. Court decisions were rare, and few were handed down against management or owners involved in workplace disasters, but isolated cases demonstrated that the courts do have legal authority to compensate injured workers. For example, on August 27, a Burmese migrant construction worker received a settlement of 100,000 baht ($3,300) for serious injuries sustained in a February 2011 work-related accident. During his suit in the Central Labor Court, the Department of Labor Protection and Welfare determined that a breach of safety regulations led to his injury.

The government continued its policy of regularizing migrant labor to help promote safe work conditions and reduce migrants' vulnerability to abuse. In addition to requiring migrants to register and undergo nationality verification, authorities instituted new registration procedures for irregular workers from Laos, Cambodia, and Burma and extended the nationality verification program through December. Under this policy authorities permit those who register to work and live temporarily in Thailand for two years and access social security and healthcare benefits. Children of registered migrants are entitled to register for residential permits if their parents have such permits. The government also reduced visa fees from 2,000 to 500 baht ($65 to $16) for each worker from Laos, Cambodia, and Burma for the next four years to incentivize workers to enter Thailand legally. As of year's end approximately 1.3 million migrant workers completed nationality verification. While there was no reliable count of irregular migrant workers in the country, governmental and NGO sources estimated the number of both regular and irregular migrant workers to be two to three million.

Migrants without documentation remained vulnerable and without recourse under the law. In order to avoid deportation, migrants often paid additional fees to police and immigration officials if caught without documentation.

As part of a broader policy to facilitate legal status for migrants, the government continued to implement procedural improvements during the year, including the establishment of five new, one-stop service centers in addition to the three existing centers already functioning informally on the Thai-Burma border. These centers helped lower the costs of travel for migrants seeking to complete the verification process by the December deadline, which authorities later extended four months to accommodate workers who did not complete the process. The government also postponed, from March 2012 to March 2013, its planned collection of repatriation funds from migrant workers in order to reduce the burden on those who comply with verification. The government provided a clear outline and detailed information on the registration process and fees, a hotline for migrant communities, a pamphlet designed to reassure relatives of migrants and border-crossing workers, and a Web site in Thai and other languages. The government also examined ways to permit migrant workers flexibility to change employers if employers mistreat migrants or violate the law.

NGOs continued to report several cases of registered migrants who had not passed nationality verification and were therefore denied accident compensation. NGOs also reported poor working conditions for both documented and undocumented migrants. Labor inspectors had limited resources, and NGOs noted concerns about the practice of giving advance warning of planned labor inspections. Civil society observers continued to criticize government handling of vulnerable migrant workers. In the Thai-Burma border area of Mae Sot, brokers often shadowed workers at Thai deportation centers and flagged their arrival at the Burmese border to procure additional fees from migrants.

Exploitative labor supply agencies persisted in charging Thai citizens working overseas large, illegal recruitment fees that frequently equaled their first- and second-year earnings. In many cases recruited workers did not receive promised benefits and incurred significant debt. NGOs noted that local moneylenders, mostly informal, continued to contribute to this practice by offering loans at exorbitant interest rates so workers could pay recruitment fees, some of which were as high as 500,000 baht ($16,400). The Ministry of Labor's Department of Employment regulations limit the maximum charges for recruitment fees, but effective enforcement of the rules remained difficult. During the year the department suspended the licenses of 43 recruitment agencies, revoked the license of one such agency, and filed criminal charges against 44 agencies.

The department also reported that, starting in June, technical support from the International Organization for Migration helped reduce the expenses and recruitment fees for Thai workers going to Israel.

In: Thailand
Editor: Kenny N. Cade
ISBN: 978-1-63117-596-1

Chapter 3

THAILAND 2012 INTERNATIONAL RELIGIOUS FREEDOM REPORT*

U.S. Department of State;
Bureau of Democracy, Human Rights and Labor

EXECUTIVE SUMMARY

The constitution and other laws and policies protect religious freedom and, in practice, the government generally respected religious freedom, although there were some reports of abuses and the government restricted the activity of certain groups. The trend in the government's respect for religious freedom did not change significantly during the year.

There were reports of societal abuses based on religious affiliation, belief or practice. In the southernmost border provinces, continued separatist violence contributed to tense relations between ethnic Thai Buddhist and ethnic Malay Muslim communities. While the conflict in the South primarily involves ethnicity and nationalism, the close affiliation between ethnic and religious identity caused it to take on religious overtones. As a result violence in the region undermined citizens' abilities to undertake the full range of their religious activities in a number of cases.

---

* This is an edited, reformatted and augmented version of a report released by the U.S. Department of State; Bureau of Democracy, Human Rights and Labor, dated May 2013.

The U.S. government discussed religious freedom with the government, visited religious leaders, hosted interreligious events, and promoted educational exchanges with the United States that supported religious freedom and tolerance.

SECTION I. RELIGIOUS DEMOGRAPHY

According to the 2010 census, the population of 66 million is 93 percent Buddhist and 5 percent Muslim. Nongovernmental organizations (NGOs), academics, and religious groups claim that 85 to 95 percent of the population is Theravada Buddhist and 5 to 10 percent is Muslim. Groups that constitute less than 5 percent of the population include animist, Christian, Confucian, Hindu, Jewish, Sikh, and Taoist populations.

Theravada Buddhism, the dominant religion, is not an exclusive belief system and most Buddhists also incorporate Brahmin-Hindu and animist practices.

The Buddhist clergy (Sangha) consists of two main schools: Mahanikaya and Dhammayuttika. The former is older and more prevalent within the monastic community than the latter. The same ecclesiastical hierarchy governs both groups.

Islam is the dominant religion in four of the five southernmost provinces. The majority of Muslims in those provinces are ethnic Malay, but the Muslim population nationally also includes descendants of immigrants from South Asia, China, Cambodia, Indonesia, and those who consider themselves ethnic Thai.

The Ministry of Interior's Islamic Affairs Section reported that, as of October, 3,744 mosques are registered in 68 of the country's 77 provinces, of which 3,179 are located in the 14 southern provinces. According to the Religious Affairs Department (RAD) of the Ministry of Culture, 99 percent of these mosques are associated with the Sunni branch of Islam. Shia mosques make up 1 percent and are in Bangkok and the provinces of Nakhon Sithammarat, Krabi, and Phatthalung. There are 39 Provincial Islamic Committees nationwide.

The majority of ethnic Chinese and Vietnamese practice Mahayana or Theravada Buddhism. Many ethnic Chinese, as well as members of the Mien hill tribe, practice forms of Taoism.

SECTION II. STATUS OF GOVERNMENT RESPECT FOR RELIGIOUS FREEDOM

Legal/Policy Framework

The constitution and other laws and policies protect religious freedom.

The 2007 constitution protects religious liberty in Section 37 and states that unjust discrimination against a person on the grounds of differences in "religious belief" shall not be permitted (Constitution Section 30). There is no significant pattern of religious discrimination by the government.

There is no state religion; however, Theravada Buddhism receives significant government support, and the 2007 constitution retains the requirement from the previous charter that the monarch be Buddhist. The constitution specifies the state shall "patronize and protect Buddhism as the religion observed by most Thais for a long period of time, as well as other religions, and shall also promote a good understanding and harmony among the followers of all religions as well as encourage the application of religious principles to create virtue and develop the quality of life."

The 2007 constitution generally provides for freedom of speech; however, laws prohibiting speech likely to insult Buddhism and other religions remain in place. The 1962 Sangha Act (amended in 1992) specifically prohibits the defamation or insult of Buddhism and the Buddhist clergy. Violators of the law can face up to one year's imprisonment or fines of up to 20,000 baht (approximately $667). The 1956 penal code's sections 206 to 208 (last amended in 1976) prohibit the insult or disturbance of religious places or services of all officially recognized religious groups. Penalties range from imprisonment of one to seven years or a fine of 2,000 to 14,000 baht ($67 to $467).

There are five officially recognized religious groups: Buddhists, Muslims, Brahmin-Hindus, Sikhs, and Christians. The RAD is responsible for registering religious groups. Under provisions of the Regulations on Religious Organizations implemented in 1969 and amended in 1982, the RAD recognizes a new religious group if a national census shows it has at least 5,000 adherents, has a uniquely recognizable theology, and is not politically active. A religious organization must also be accepted into at least one of the five existing recognized religious groups before the RAD will grant registration. Generally, the government requires that new groups receive acceptance from existing groups with similar belief systems. Government registration confers some benefits, including access to state subsidies, tax exempt status, and preferential allocation of resident visas for organization officials; however, since 1984 the government has not recognized any new religious groups. In practice unregistered religious groups operate freely, and the government's practice of not recognizing any new religious groups does not restrict their activities.

The law requires religious education at both the primary and secondary levels. In 2003 the Ministry of Education introduced a course called "Social, Religion, and Culture Studies," which students in each grade study for one to two hours each week. The course contains information about all of the recognized religious groups in the country. Students who wish to pursue in-depth studies of a particular religion may study at a religious school and can transfer credits to the public school. Individual schools, working in conjunction with their local administrative boards, are authorized to arrange additional religious studies courses. The Supreme Sangha Council and the Central Islamic Committee of Thailand create special curriculums for Buddhist and Islamic studies.

There are four types of Islamic educational institutions in the southern part of the country. The first comprises government-subsidized schools. This type of schooling offers Islamic education in conjunction with the national curriculum. The language of instruction is Thai, and there are approximately 271 schools in this category. The government recognizes these schools, supports them financially, and graduating students can continue to higher education within the country.

The second type consists of private Islamic schools. There are approximately 202 schools in this category. In 2003 the government encouraged these schools to adopt a government-approved Islamic studies curriculum. Some private Islamic schools may offer non-Quranic subjects such as foreign languages (Arabic and English). These schools usually register with the government. Students finishing their studies under this curriculum may become eligible to pursue higher education if they take a state comparability examination.

The third type, traditional pondoks, or private Islamic day schools, offer Islamic education to students of all ages. Each school chooses its own curriculum, which has traditionally been built around the teacher, often the local imam or founder. The language of instruction at many pondoks is Malay. Many of these schools do not register with the government. Since they are unregistered, the exact number of traditional pondoks in the country is unknown. Estimates range from 328-1,000. Students graduating from unregistered pondoks do not receive automatic government certification of their studies. They are, however, able to take a compatibility exam that compares their knowledge to the government-approved Islamic Studies curriculum. Those who pass this exam receive government certification.

Finally, a tadika is an after-school religious course for children in grades one through six, which often is held in a mosque. The RAD is responsible for overseeing the program, except in the southernmost provinces of Satun, Narathiwat, Yala, Pattani, and parts of Songkhla, where the Ministry of Education supervises courses.

The government observes the following religious holidays as national holidays: Maka Bucha Day (the full moon day of the third lunar month, typically in February); Visakha Bucha Day (the full moon day of the sixth lunar month, typically in May); Asalaha Bucha Day (the full moon day of the eighth lunar month, typically in July); and Khao Phan Sa Day (beginning of the Buddhist Lent, typically during the summer).

Government Practices

There were reports of abuses of religious freedom in the country. Pattaya Tourist Police reportedly arrested a group of five Falun Gong practitioners in December 2011 for trespass and nuisance while they were distributing leaflets. The five were reportedly released, with no new information of further legal action against them in 2012. The Ministry of Interior (MOI) denied Falun Gong representatives' request to register officially as a foundation or association. Falun Gong leaders petitioned the Administrative Court to reverse the denial, but the court concurred with the MOI. The ruling was appealed to the Supreme Administrative Court and remained pending at year's end.

In March 2009 Nima Kaseng, wife of Imam Yapa Kaseng, filed a civil suit against the Ministry of Defense, the army, and the police demanding 12,285,530 baht (approximately $410,000) in compensation after the December 2008 Narathiwat Provincial Court ruled that Imam Yapa was killed in March 2008 while in military custody. The three defendants agreed to settle the civil case for 5.2 million baht ($173,000) in July 2011. The Supreme Court of Justice closed its inquiry into the question of military or civilian court jurisdiction over criminal charges when the lower court that originally denied civilian jurisdiction did not certify the associated petition. The military court criminal case remained inactive pending the concurrent administrative investigation by the National Counter Corruption Commission, which reported no progress in 2012.

During the year, the government instituted several compensation programs for victims of southern violence with payments up to 7.5 million baht (approximately $250,000).

The government did not recognize religious groups other than the five existing registered communities; however, unregistered religious organizations operated freely.

The 2007 constitution required that the government "patronize and protect Buddhism and other religions." In accordance with this requirement, the government subsidized activities of all five primary religious communities. The government allocated 4.3 billion baht (approximately $143 million) for fiscal year 2012 to support the National Buddhism Bureau, an independent state agency. The bureau oversees the Buddhist clergy and approves the curriculums of Buddhist teachings for all Buddhist temples and educational institutions. In addition, the bureau sponsored educational and public relations materials on Buddhism as it relates to daily life. During the year the government budgeted 365 million baht ($12.2 million) for the RAD, including 190 million baht ($6.3 million) for Buddhist organizations; 36 million baht ($1.2 million) for Islamic organizations; and 2.1 million baht ($70,000) for Christian, Brahmin-Hindu, and Sikh organizations. The RAD fiscal year budget also allocated 28.5 million baht ($950,000) for religious lectures, 96 million baht ($3.2 million) for Buddhist Sunday school, 12 million baht ($400,000) for Islamic study centers, 7.5 million baht ($250,000) for religious activities for persons with disabilities, and 4.6 million baht ($153,000) for interfaith events. Pursuant to the Hajj Pilgrimage Promotion Act of 1981, the government budgeted 16.1 million baht ($537,000) for the year, down from 19 million baht ($613,000) the previous year, to promote and facilitate Muslim participation in the Hajj pilgrimage.

In areas of the southern provinces where violence has occurred, the government continued to provide armed escorts for Buddhist monks for their daily rounds to receive alms and during Buddhist festivals. Government troops also continued to station themselves within Buddhist temples, which some NGOs and ethnic Malay Muslims perceived as a militarization of Buddhist temples. Other NGOs viewed the military presence as a response to the prior attacks on Buddhist temples. Some temples declined to have military protection, both to avoid militants targeting them and due to the perceived costs, such as higher utility bills and the effort involved in controlling behavior on temple grounds. Many temples therefore preferred to rely on Buddhist volunteers for security.

The budgets for Buddhist and Islamic organizations included funds to support Buddhist and Islamic institutes of higher education, to fund religious education programs in public and private schools, to provide daily allowances for monks and Muslim clerics who hold administrative and senior ecclesiastical posts, and to subsidize travel and health care for monks and Muslim clerics. They also included an annual budget for the renovation and repair of temples and mosques, the maintenance of historic Buddhist sites, and the daily upkeep of the central mosque in Pattani. The National Buddhism Bureau allocated 392 million baht ($13.1 million) for the maintenance of Buddhist temples and institutions.

Other registered religious groups can request government support for renovation and repair work but do not receive a regular budget to maintain religious buildings, nor do they receive government assistance to support their clergy. During the year the RAD budgeted 20 million baht ($667,000) for the restoration of 891 religious buildings of non-Buddhist religious groups. The RAD budget for the maintenance of religious buildings remained unchanged from the previous year. Private donations to registered religious organizations are tax deductible.

Religious groups generally proselytized freely. Monks working as dhammaduta (Buddhist missionaries) were active, particularly in border areas among the country's tribal populations. According to the National Buddhism Bureau, there were 5,391 appointed dhammaduta working nationwide. In addition, the government appointed approximately 2,100 dhammaduta for international travel, and 1,481 were overseas working in 37 countries. There were 369 registered Thai Buddhist temples abroad, located in 32 countries. In 2009 the Supreme Sangha Council and the National Buddhism Bureau recruited more than 400 recently graduated monks with religious degrees to work in the provinces on four-year tenured contracts as part of a domestic religious dissemination program. The program continued, but recruitment of monks to fill new vacancies was suspended in 2012.

Muslim and Christian missionaries did not receive public funds or state subsidies. Islamic organizations had small numbers of citizens working as missionaries in the country and abroad. Christian organizations had much larger numbers of missionaries, both foreign and Thai, across all denominations operating in the country. Sikhs and Hindu-Brahmins had smaller numbers reflecting their proportion of the population.

In 1982 the RAD limited the number of foreign missionaries registered with the government to an official quota organized along both religious and denominational lines.

The RAD increased the missionary quota for a few religious groups in recent years. There were close to 1,600 registered foreign missionaries in the country, mostly Christian. In addition to these formal quotas, many unregistered missionaries lived and worked in the country without government interference. While registration conferred some benefits, such as visas with longer validity, being unregistered was not a significant barrier to foreign missionary activity. Many foreign missionaries entered the country using tourist visas and proselytized without RAD's authorization. There were no reports that the government deported or harassed foreign missionaries for working without registration.

Muslim professors and clerics, particularly in the southernmost provinces, faced additional scrutiny because of continuing government concern about Malay Muslim separatist activities. While this usually did not appear to inhibit their religious activities, government officials continued to be concerned that some Islamic schools indoctrinated youth into the conflict. Conversely, some reports concluded that southern insurgents targeted state schools and teachers because they perceived them to be part of an effort to impose Thai Buddhist culture on the region (see Section III, below, which notes violence against school personnel).

A clause in the 2007 constitution required the government to "promote good understanding and harmony among followers of all religions." In accordance with this clause, the government sponsored interfaith dialogue through regular meetings and public education programs. The RAD carried out and oversaw many of these efforts.

On August 25-26, the RAD held its annual interfaith assembly in Chiang Rai, and approximately 1,000 representatives and members of all registered religious groups participated. The RAD, in conjunction with provincial authorities, also sponsored Youth Reconciliation Camps in 62 provinces throughout the country. Each event lasted two to three days and drew at least 100 participants from all major religious groups in each province, mostly students in grades 10-12. The goals of the camps were to create and strengthen mutual religious understanding through activities, games, religious classes, and interaction. The camp in the southern province of Songkhla drew approximately 300 participants.

SECTION III. STATUS OF SOCIETAL RESPECT FOR RELIGIOUS FREEDOM

There were reports of societal abuses and discrimination based on religious affiliation, belief, or practice. Ethnicity and religion are often inextricably linked; for this reason it is difficult to categorize many incidents specifically as ethnic or religious intolerance. While the conflict in the South was primarily about ethnicity and nationalism, the close connection between ethnic and religious identity caused it to take on religious overtones. Violence perpetrated by ethnic Malay Muslims against ethnic Thai Buddhists in the southernmost provinces exacerbated tensions and invited retaliatory killings and human rights abuses by both groups. As a result, in a number of cases the violence in the region undermined the ability of citizens to practice the full range of their religious activities.

Insurgents continued high-profile attacks during the holy month of Ramadan with at least 99 incidents during the month killing 52 and injuring 98 others. For the first time in the conflict, insurgents used at least three 50kg bombs during Ramadan, a substantial increase from the 20kg bombs used to date. During the first week of Ramadan attacks killed at least nine persons and injured 28: on July 20, a 50kg bomb exploded as a military unit drove by in an armored truck, injuring seven soldiers and one Muslim villager in Narathiwat Province. On July 25, five policemen in a patrol squad in Yala Province died after a 50kg improvised explosive device (IED) detonated as their unit passed. Another 50 kg bomb exploded behind a popular hotel in Pattani city on July 31, injuring five persons. A surveillance camera captured the most brazen attack in Pattani Province, which was later leaked to the press: a group of at least 16 insurgents in three trucks shot and killed four paramilitary rangers on motorcycles and injured two others and then stole their weapons.

At least one imam was killed: two gunmen on a motorcycle shot and killed Imam Abdullateh Todir, Chairman of the Imam Association in Amphoe Yaha and a member of the Yala Provincial Islamic Committee, on November 14 while he drove his pick-up truck. After his death and the fatal shooting of a Muslim teacher on October 30, insurgents put Buddhist teachers back on their hit list, and shot and killed four teachers between November 22 and December 11. Before these incidents, the government provided most teachers with security escorts for their travel to and from work. After these incidents, authorities increased security measures for teachers in highly sensitive areas and offered them around-the-clock protection.

As in previous years, Buddhist monks continued to report they were fearful and thus no longer able to travel freely through southern communities to receive alms or perform rites. As a safety precaution, they often conducted religious rites customarily performed in the evening in the afternoon instead. A roadside bomb injured two monks in Pattani Province when it exploded while they collected morning alms on June 9. The same explosion also injured three members of their military escort and two Buddhist villagers.

There were reports of several incidents involving intimidation and violence by unidentified attackers against peaceful Falun Gong protesters, some near the embassy of China, but no arrests were reported.

On January 10, an estimated 400 demonstrators gathered at Government House, the executive office complex for the prime minister and cabinet, to protest the decision by Wat Nong Chok Secondary School in Bangkok prohibiting female students from wearing headscarves at school. The Ministry of Education attempted to negotiate a compromise, but the school's abbot refused to end the ban.

On November 11, in an apparently isolated incident, a group of approximately 20 Buddhist villagers in Udon Thani province stormed a Christian church and destroyed its contents, allegedly in reaction to the church's proselytizing activities.

Section IV. U.S. Government Policy

U.S. embassy officers and high-level visitors from the Department of State discussed religious freedom with the government. They regularly visited Muslim and Buddhist religious leaders, academics, and elected officials as part of the embassy's effort to promote religious freedom and to understand the complex ethnic and religious issues at play in society.

Both the embassy and the U.S. consulate general in Chiang Mai hosted iftars (dinners during the month of Ramadan) to demonstrate respect for, and an understanding of, Islamic traditicns, and to share information about Muslim life in the United States as well as the importance of religious freedom. During Ramadan, a local Muslim magazine interviewed the ambassador and featured the interview on the cover of the issue published during the month. The ambassador met with the newly appointed Apostolic Nuncio to Thailand and Cambodia and hosted a large reception celebrating diversity in Thailand. The guests included a wide range of religious leaders. The embassy organized several other cultural programs, including events focusing specifically on religious freedom and tolerance or on the predominantly Muslim southern regions, such as digital video conferences with American Corners in the south to promote study in the U.S. and English-language skills development.

The embassy also sponsored a speaker who talked about her life as a female Muslim American. The speaker met with various Muslim groups throughout the country, including students, community leaders, and a Muslim women's group. She also met with the leadership of the Songkhla Central Islamic Committee and Mosque. That mosque, the country's largest, also serves as a cultural center and Islamic administrative center in the south, the region with the highest population of Muslim citizens.

The Department of State's under secretary for civilian security, democracy, and human rights engaged Muslim youth at an event with the Chiang Mai Muslim Student Society. After touring Hedaytul Islam Mosque, the under secretary held a youth roundtable discussion with 25 young people to discuss activities and challenges facing the 15,000 Muslims in Chiang Mai. The under secretary took the opportunity to highlight U.S. initiatives to engage youth and strengthen relationships with Muslim communities. Officers from the consulate general in Chiang Mai participated in several interreligious events organized by the Chiang Mai Interreligious Relations Committee.

In: Thailand
Editor: Kenny N. Cade

ISBN: 978-1-63117-596-1

Chapter 4

2013 INVESTMENT CLIMATE STATEMENT: THAILAND*

Bureau of Economic and Business Affairs

OPENNESS TO FOREIGN INVESTMENT

Despite internal political tensions and severe flooding in 2011, Thailand continues to maintain an open, market-oriented economy and encourages foreign direct investment as a means of promoting economic development, employment, and technology transfer. In recent decades, Thailand has been a major destination for foreign direct investment, and hundreds of U.S. companies have invested in Thailand successfully. Thailand continues to welcome investment from all countries and seeks to avoid dependence on any one country as a source of investment. Following the significant impact of flooding in late 2011, investors are seeking development and implementation of an improved government water management plan as a critical element to maintaining investor confidence.

With flooding affecting 60 of 77 provinces, especially manufacturers in key industrial estates in Bangkok and its five surrounding provinces, a sharp contraction of nearly 9 percent occurred in the fourth quarter, wiping out 3.2 percent (year-on-year) growth during the first three quarters to only a mere 0.1 percent for the 2011 full-year GDP. However, the Thai economy remains

* This is an edited, reformatted and augmented version of Bureau of Economic and Business Affairs publication, dated February 2013.

resilient in the face of the severe domestic floods and continuing global economic crises. After the flat growth in 2011, recovery from the floods was satisfyingly rapid during the first three quarters of 2012 (2.6 percent) due to robust domestic demand from reconstruction and the government's stimulus programs. With low base effect during the last quarter, the government anticipated the 2012 full-year growth at a rate of 5.5 percent. Concerns over fleeing foreign investors out of the country also proved largely unfounded.

In the wake of the 1997-98 Asian Financial Crisis, Thailand embarked on an International Monetary Fund (IMF)-sponsored economic reform program designed to foster a more competitive and transparent climate for foreign investors. Legislation in 1999 established a new bankruptcy court, reformed bankruptcy, and foreclosure procedures, and allowed creditors to pursue payment from loan guarantors. Other 1999 reforms include amendments to the Land Code, Condominium Act, and the Property Leasing Act, all of which liberalized restrictions on property ownership by non-Thais. The Foreign Business Act (FBA) of 1999 continues to govern most investment activity by non-Thai nationals. The FBA opened some additional business sectors to foreign investment; however, foreign investment in most service sectors is limited to 49 percent ownership. Other key laws governing foreign investment are Alien Employment Act B.E. 2521 (1978) and Investment Promotion Act B.E. 2520 (1977).

Foreign companies are free to open and maintain bank accounts in foreign currency. However, Thailand retains to some extent its investment control, as under certain circumstances, foreign investors that are previously granted national treatment are subject to some reservations, in particular the service sector. From January 2012, the lower corporate tax rate was reduced from 30 percent to 23 percent, and will be cut further to 20 percent from January 2013 onward. Benefits of the lower corporate tax rate, however, may be offset by an increase of daily minimum wage rate of around 40 percent in April 2012 and by another 22.4 percent to a uniform Thai Baht300 per day ($10) in January 2013 nationwide.

U.S. Investment

Many U.S. businesses enjoy investment benefits through the U.S.-Thailand Treaty of Amity and Economic Relations (AER), originally signed in 1833. The 1966 iteration of the Treaty allows U.S. citizens and businesses incorporated in the U.S., or in Thailand that are majority-owned by U.S.

citizens, to engage in business on the same basis as Thai companies (national treatment), exempting them from most restrictions on foreign investment imposed by the Foreign Business Act. Under the Treaty, American investment is restricted only in the fields of communications, transport, fiduciary functions, banking involving depository functions, the exploitation of land or other natural resources, and domestic trade in agricultural products. Prospective U.S. investors who seek benefits from the Treaty must first verify their nationality by obtaining a certified letter from the U.S. Embassy in Bangkok. For the representative office and foreign branch, the process stops at the U.S. Embassy, but for the investor wishing to register in Thailand in the form of company limited, the investor must then present the Embassy's letter to the Ministry of Commerce, along with an application form for a business operation certificate. This process typically takes less than one month.

Notwithstanding their Treaty rights, many Americans choose to form joint ventures with Thai partners, allowing the Thai side to hold the majority stake because of the advantages that come from familiarity with the Thai economy and local regulations.

Americans planning to invest in Thailand are advised to obtain qualified legal advice. Such advice is particularly important given the fact that Thai business regulations are governed predominantly by criminal, not civil law. While foreigners rarely are jailed for improper business activities, violation of Thai business regulations can carry heavy criminal penalties.

Banking

Thailand has removed some barriers to foreign ownership of domestic financial institutions. Meanwhile the establishment of new branches of foreign banks is subject to licensing, but in practice, foreign banks' only channel to market access during the past decades is through acquisition of shares of existing domestic banks. The Financial Institutions Act, passed at the end of 2007, unified the legal framework and strengthened Bank of Thailand (the country's central bank) supervision and enforcement powers. The Act gave power to the Bank of Thailand to raise the foreign ownership limit in a local bank from 25 percent to 49 percent on a case-by-case basis, as currently there is no policy for giving out new banking licenses. The Act also allows the Minister of Finance to authorize foreign ownership above 49 percent only if recommended by the central bank. In January 2009, the Ministry of Finance allowed Malaysia's CIMB Group to hold majority shares (around 93 percent) in BankThai, the country's ninth largest commercial bank, changing its name to CIMB Thai Bank Public Company Limited. In February 2010, the Ministry of Finance also granted Industrial and Commercial Bank of China (ICBC - the largest commercial bank in China) a waiver for the 49 percent foreign ownership limit to 97.24 percent in ACL Bank, Thailand's smallest commercial bank, renaming it as ICBC (Thai) Public Company Limited. The other two are Nakornthon Bank, with England's Standard Chartered Group, holding 99.87 percent ownership and the new name Standard Chartered Bank (Thai) Public Company Limited, and Bank of Asia with Singaporean United Overseas Bank as a majority holder (99.66 percent ownership), called UOB (Thai) Public Company Limited. The increase of foreign participation in the Thai banking system has improved competitiveness in the sector.

Thailand continues to implement the terms of its five-year (2010-2014) Financial Sector Master Plan Phase II (FSMP II) with the objective of comprehensive risk management, cost reduction, and enhancing competitiveness in the banking system with the possibility of opening up new banking licenses in 2014. FSMP Phase I (2004-2008) was concluded in 2008 with the focus on strengthening Thai banking sector through the policies of consolidation. The objective of implementation of the FSMP is to get the banking sector ready for more open economy. Beginning in 2012, the Bank of Thailand will permit foreign banks to upgrade existing full branches to 'subsidiaries,' which will allow foreign banks to open up to 20 branches and 20 off-premise ATMs across Thailand. Qualifying branches must maintain a capital adequacy ratio of no less than 12 percent, compared with a domestic minimum requirement of 8.5 percent, and non-performing loans must be kept under 3.5 percent. In addition, the converted subsidiary must have a minimum of $333 million in paid-up-capital. As of December 2012, there were 31 commercial banks, including 14 locally incorporated commercial banks, 1 retail bank, 15 foreign bank branches, including three American banks (Citibank, Bank of America, and JP Morgan Chase), and one subsidiary operating in Thailand. Beginning in March 2010, existing foreign bank branches have been permitted to request opening up to two additional branches in Thailand without having to meet additional capital requirements. Details of the FSMP II are available in English at: http://www.bot.or.th/. In addition, under the new Basel III capital framework starting on January 2013, foreign bank branches will be required to maintain a minimum total capital ratio of 8.5 percent, in line with Thai banks.

The Thai banking sector is profitable, strong, well-capitalized, and has sound risk management. During the first three quarters of 2012, the banking system recorded US$4.5 billion in net profit, growing by 19.0 percent from the same period of the previous year. Despite the worst flooding in a century in late 2011, major rating agencies provided a stable outlook for the Thai banking sector, citing temporary economic impact from the floods and noting that the fundamentals of Thai banks remain robust. After peaking at 47 percent of total lending in May 1999 from the financial crisis, net non-performing loans slowly declined to stand at 1.2 percent of total loans in September 2012. Capital Adequacy Ratio (BIS ratio) and Tier-1 ratio of the domestic banks registered at 15.9 percent and 11.9 percent, respectively in the third quarter of 2012. Total assets of the country's largest six banks stood at 10.6 trillion Thai baht (approximately US$355 billion) or roughly 90 percent of GDP as of September 2012.

Insurance

The 2008 Life Insurance Act and the 2008 Non-Life Insurance Act apply a 25 percent cap on foreign ownership of insurance companies and on foreign directors of boards. However, the Office of the Insurance Commission (OIC) may, at its discretion, permit foreign equity ownership up to 49 percent, and foreign directorship up to 50 percent. Foreign ownership restrictions may be relaxed further in cases where the Minister of Finance, upon recommendation from the OIC, determines that financial problems at an insurance company may cause damage to the insured or the general public. The Acts also stipulate that limited liability and non-life insurance companies are required to be registered as public companies by 2013, though listing on the Stock Exchange of Thailand is not a requirement. Companies that fail to comply by 2013 will be unable to open new branches and can be fined up to 200,000 Thai baht (approximately US$6,000) plus daily fines of up to 10,000 Thai baht (approximately US$300).

Business Registration

Any entity wishing to do business in Thailand must register with the Department of Business Development at the Ministry of Commerce, generally taking from three to six months to complete. Firms engaging in production activities need to register with the Ministries of Industry and Labor and Social Welfare. If the entity falls under the definition of non-Thai national as defined by the Foreign Business Act, they have to obtain a 'foreign business license' (or a certificate for US investors as mentioned above), which must be approved by the Council of Ministers (Cabinet) or Director-General of Department of Business Development at the Ministry of Commerce depending on types of restricted businesses.

Work Permits

Thai law requires foreign workers to have a work permit issued by the Ministry of Labor in order to work legally in Thailand; Thai law also reserves 39 occupations for Thai workers and will not grant work permits for foreigners to engage in these occupations, including lawyers, architects, and civil engineers. Foreigners found to be working without work permits could be imprisoned up to five years and/or fined between 2,000 and 100,000 Thai baht (approximately US$60 to US$3,000). Exceptions to the requirement for a work permit include officially recognized diplomatic and consular delegations, representatives of member countries and officials of the United Nations and specialized institutions, personal servants working for the above persons, and those who are performing duties or missions otherwise exempted by the Royal Thai Government. Volunteer or charity work can be considered work under Thai law, requiring a work permit.

Factors that influence the granting of work permits include the degree of specialization required by the position, the size of the firm in terms of number of employees and registered capitalization, and the ratio of Thai nationals to foreigners employed by the firm. Foreigners working for the Thai government or working on projects promoted by the Board of Investment (BOI) usually have little difficulty obtaining work permits and typically receive their permits within seven days of application. Work permits in other areas are sometimes difficult to obtain. The duration of work permits is generally tied to the length of stay permitted by the person's visa.

U.S. citizens can enter Thailand without a visa for visits of up to thirty days. In order to apply for a work permit, a foreigner must enter Thailand on a non-immigrant visa (issued at Thai embassies and consulates) for a stay of three months or, for foreigners with well-defined work or business plans, for a stay of one year. Issuance of the three-month visa usually is completed within two or three days; the one-year visa requires approval from the Immigration Bureau of the Royal Thai Police in Bangkok. Upon obtaining a work permit, a holder of a three-month visa may apply for a one-year visa, which generally can be extended every year. Foreigners holding nonimmigrant visas who have lived in Thailand for at least three consecutive years may apply for permanent residence in Thailand if they meet strict criteria regarding investment or professional skills.

Land Ownership

In general, non-Thai businesses and citizens are not permitted to own land in Thailand unless the land is on government-approved industrial estates. Under the 1999 amendment to the Land Code Act, foreigners who invest a minimum of 40 million Baht (approximately US$1.3 million) are permitted to buy up to 1,600 square meters of land for residential use with the permission of the Ministry of Interior. If the required land is not used as a residence within two years from the date of acquisition and registration, the Ministry has the power to dispose of the land. Petroleum concessionaires may own land necessary for their activities. Rather than purchasing, many foreign businesses instead sign long-term leases, and then construct buildings on the leased land. Under the 1999 Condominium Act, non-Thais were allowed to own up to 100 percent of a condominium building if they purchased the unit between April 28, 1999 and April 28, 2004. Under the newer Condominium Act of 2007, foreign ownership in a condominium building, when added together, must not exceed 49 percent of the total space of all units in the building, except for those purchased between 1999 and 2004.

Privatization

With the aim of encouraging capital inflows and relieving resource constraints in many key sectors of the economy, the previous government of Thaksin Shinawatra embarked on a privatization program for state-owned economic enterprises and state monopolies. The interim government that followed the September 2006 coup as well as the former government of Abhisit Vejjajiva (Democrat party) considered privatization too controversial and put these plans on hold. Most privatization plans have remained on hold since. Other than the Petroleum Authority of Thailand (PTT), the Airport Authority of Thailand (later renamed Airports of Thailand (AOT) and the Mass Communication Organization of Thailand (MCOT), few significant privatizations have occurred. The 1999 State Enterprise Corporatization Act provides the framework for the conversion of state enterprises into stock companies, and corporatization is viewed as an intermediate step toward eventual privatization. (Note: "Corporatization" describes the process by which an SOE adjusts its internal structure to resemble a publicly-traded enterprise; "privatization" means that a majority of the SOE's shares is sold to the public, and "partial privatization" refers to a situation in which less than half a company's shares are sold to the public.) Foreign investors are allowed to participate in the privatization but certain restrictions are also applied in certain sectors, which mostly regulated by the Foreign Business Act of 1999 and the Act on Standards Qualifications for Directors and Employees of State Enterprises of 1975 and its series of amendments. The current State Enterprise Policy Office under the Ministry of Finance does not have the power to regulate all SOEs. Meanwhile, a draft comprehensive bill to set up a new regulatory and policy body to supervise all SOEs, including those that have been partially privatized, remains stalled.

International Rankings

The following is a summary of Thailand's rankings in several international indexes, as well as the Millennium Challenge Corporation's (MCC) score card.

Measure	Year	Index/Ranking
TI Corruption Index	2012	37/88
Heritage Economic Freedom	2012	64.9/60
World Bank Doing Business	October 2012	18

Note: The MCC Index no longer applies for Thailand. In July 2011, the World Bank upgraded Thailand from a Lower Middle Income Country to an Upper Middle Income Country.

CONVERSION AND TRANSFER POLICIES

All foreign exchange transactions must be conducted through commercial banks and authorized non-banks, namely money changers, money transfer agents, and companies that are granted foreign exchange licenses by the Minister of Finance. Inward remittances are free of controls. Repatriation of investment funds and repayment of overseas loans can be remitted freely but only upon submission of supporting documents to commercial banks, including evidence of sale or transfer in the case of investment funds and evidence of inward remittance supporting the loan agreement.

Thai nationals are subject to quantitative limits on the amount of foreign currency that can be remitted abroad without specific permission from the Bank of Thailand. The limits vary depending upon the purpose of the transaction, and range from US$100 million per annum for business investment or loans to subsidiaries, to US$1 million per annum for remittances to family members. The Bank of Thailand must approve the purchase of immovable assets or securities abroad, except the latest exemption mentioned above. The new regulation, however, also increases the limit of overseas fund remittances in foreign currencies up to US$1 million by Thai individual. In addition, the authorities relaxed the repatriation requirement for exporters with foreign currency receipts by extending the period in which such receipts must be brought into the country from within 120 days, to within 360 days and requiring that the foreign currencies be deposited or sold with financial institutions within another 360 days. In 2010, the repatriation requirement is exempted if the export proceeds are less than US$50,000. A person traveling to any of Thailand's border countries (and Vietnam) may take up to 500,000 Baht (US$16,600), and up to 50,000 Baht (US$1,660) for other countries, without prior authorization.

Commercial banks are authorized to undertake most routine foreign remittance transactions without prior approval from the Bank of Thailand. Non-residents can open and maintain foreign currency accounts without deposit and withdrawal ceilings with authorized banks in Thailand. Such accounts must use funds that originate abroad. If non-residents have underlying liabilities or transactions in Thailand, they can open and maintain Thai baht accounts under Non-resident Baht Accounts (NRBA) with authorized banks in the country; however, the combined outstanding of all NRBAs for each non-resident at the end of the day cannot exceed 300 million baht (approximately US$9 million). Since February 2008, the Bank of Thailand has segregated the NRBA into two types: Non-resident Baht Account for Securities (NRBS) for investment in securities and other financial instruments, and Non-resident Baht Account (NRBA) for general purposes. Funds under the two types of NRBA cannot be transferred to the other. The cap on NRBAs was introduced in October 2003 with the goal of limiting speculation on the Thai baht. All remittances exceeding US$10,000 for any purpose other than export must be reported to the Bank of Thailand.

In general, foreign currencies may be brought into Thailand and are not subject to quantitative limits. Any person who brings foreign currencies into or out of Thailand exceeding US$20,000 or the equivalent must declare the amount at a Customs checkpoint. Foreigners staying in Thailand for less than three months, as well as those working for foreign embassies and international organizations, are exempt from this requirement.

Due to the substantial appreciation of the Thai baht in 2010, the Ministry of Finance and the Bank of Thailand relaxed regulations on capital outflows. The changes included allowing Thai export companies to transfer funds from their foreign currency deposit accounts to counterparties in Thailand for payment of goods and services without exchanging into Thai baht, and increasing the foreign exchange transactions threshold amount for which a foreign exchange transaction form must be submitted from US$20,000 to US$50,000. The Ministry of Finance abolished the US$200 million per year limit of lending and direct investment of Thai companies to affiliated companies abroad, and relaxed the pre-approval requirement for all transactions of Thai companies' lending to non-affiliated companies abroad to only transactions above US$50 million per year. The government also increased the limit for purchase of immovable properties abroad from US$5 million per year to US$10 million per year; raised the outstanding balance limit of foreign currency accounts that are deposited with funds converted from Thai baht without future obligations with commercial banks in the country to US$500,000 for both companies and individuals; abolished a pre-approval requirement on unwinding of foreign exchange hedging transactions for goods and services; and relaxed regulations on corporate treasury centers on both lending, deposit and fund transfer activities.

In 2007, the Bank of Thailand and the Ministry of Finance doubled the ceiling on foreign currency deposited with financial institutions in the country from US$0.5 million to US$1 million for individuals and from US$50 million to US$100 million for juristic persons with future foreign exchange obligations within the following 12 months. The deposit ceiling applies only to foreign currencies that are borrowed from financial institutions, but if foreign currencies are earned (not borrowed), the deposit ceiling restriction is not applied.

Expropriation and Compensation

Private property can be expropriated for public purposes in accordance with Thai law, which provides for due process and compensation. In practice, this process is seldom used and has been principally confined to real estate owned by Thai nationals and needed for public works projects. U.S. firms have not reported any problems with property appropriation in Thailand.

Dispute Settlement

Thailand has a civil code, commercial code, and a bankruptcy law. Monetary judgments are calculated at the market exchange rate. Decisions of foreign courts are not accepted or enforceable in Thai courts. Disputes such as the enforcement of property or contract rights have generally been resolved through the Thai courts. Thailand has an independent judiciary that generally is effective in enforcing property and contractual rights. The legal process is slow in practice, however, and litigants or third parties sometimes affect judgments through extra-legal means.

In addition, companies may establish their own arbitration agreements. Thailand signed the Convention on the Settlement of Investment Disputes Between States and Nationals of Other States in 1985, but has not yet ratified the Convention. Thailand is a member of the New York Convention and enacted its own rules on conciliation and arbitration in the Arbitration Act of 2002. The 2002 Arbitration Act adopted the principles under the United Nations Commission on International Trade Law (UNCITRAL). The Arbitration Office of the Ministry of Justice administers these procedures.

The Bankruptcy Act was amended in 1999 to provide Chapter 11-style protection to debtors, and to give debtors and creditors the option of negotiating a reorganization plan through the courts instead of forcing liquidation. The Act now allows creditors to extend additional loans to insolvent firms without losing the right to claim compensation during a future restructuring or liquidation process, but only if the new loan is intended to keep the firm in operation. Also in 1999, the Act was amended to facilitate the financial restructuring process. Higher minimum levels for individual and corporate bankruptcies were established, and the previous ten-year period of bankruptcy status was reduced to three years. The 1999 Bankruptcy Act also established a specialized court for bankruptcy cases. The Bankruptcy Courts are divided into the Central Bankruptcy Court which has jurisdiction throughout the Bangkok Metropolitan areas and the Regional Bankruptcy Courts.

In 2004, Parliament approved changes to the Bankruptcy Act including tightening the rules under which some debtors can emerge from bankruptcy status and streamlining the legal appeals process in bankruptcy and restructuring cases. In an effort to quicken the foreclosure process, amendments to the Civil Procedure Code on Execution of Judgments have limited appeal options available to debtors. Under the old regulations, debtors were free to appeal each action taken with respect to the execution of a bankruptcy judgment. Such appeals, often frivolous in nature, were one of the tactics debtors used to delay the foreclosure process. In June 2001, the Supreme Court set an important legal precedent by ruling in favor of implementing a creditor-backed corporate restructuring plan opposed by the former owner of the business in question. The Act was later amended in 2005 by granting the Bankruptcy Court the power to consider bankruptcy cases that involve criminal matters.

Individual cases can take months, or even years, to work their way through the legal system however, and many businesses have urged the government to speed up the bankruptcy procedure. In 2006, new procedural rules were established to accelerate the bankruptcy court proceedings by encouraging the use of electronic equipment and express mail in communications between courts. Under the new rules, provincial courts have the authority to issue search warrants and arrest warrants, and to imprison or release a defendant. Other amendments to the Bankruptcy Act are currently under consideration.

In 2009, the Bankruptcy Court issued verdicts on 33,055 cases. (More current statistics are not available.)

PERFORMANCE REQUIREMENTS AND INCENTIVES

WTO TRIMS

Thailand committed to implement all WTO agreements, including Trade-Related Investment Measures (TRIMS). In its latest Trade Policy Review in November 2011, the WTO noted, "Thailand did not take any new measures to restrict trade since the 2008 global financial crisis. Indeed, it has made some important improvements to trading conditions in some areas, such as its adoption of paperless import procedures and its intention to move to a single [customs] window. Furthermore, an appeals system has been introduced by the Customs Department to cover many aspects of import procedures. As a member of ASEAN, Thailand has adopted the Association's harmonized tariff nomenclature which has also helped facilitate trade by standardizing the customs codes used to identify products."

The report also said that Thailand has committed to liberalize the regulatory regime with legislation governing key sectors such as transport, distribution, and telecommunications under review. However, the report observed that there are some areas of Thailand's import and domestic policies that could hamper trading opportunities and impede its development, including agriculture policies such as domestic support and tariff quota administration, complex tariffs structure, technical barriers to trade and Sanitary Phyto Sanitary (SPS) measures, and intellectual property. The report also underlined that despite progress in the liberalization of trade in some service sectors, there remain concerns over foreign ownership and market access restrictions in financial services (particularly the insurance sector), telecommunications, maritime and professional services. The report noted that Thailand has yet to modify its General Agreement on Trade in Services (GATS) schedule following the negotiations on telecommunications in 1997.

Investment Incentives

The Board of Investment (BOI), established by the Investment Promotion Act of 1977, is Thailand's central investment promotion authority. The BOI offers investment incentives uniformly to both qualified domestic and foreign investors with a clear articulation of the application procedures. Good governance is one of the key factors to manage and supervise the application for tax and duty privileges. Complete information on BOI's updated policies, programs, incentives, and application procedures can be found on the BOI web site at: www.boi.go.th.

In November 2009, BOI established the 'One Start One Stop Investment Center' as a centralized location to assist investors with the requirements of the various investment related government agencies. Staff at the Center provide guidance to investors on how to register a company, obtain BOI's investment promotion privileges, obtain a foreign business license, complete an environmental impact assessment, request permission to use land for industrial operations, obtain utilities, and other related investment issues. More information could be found on its web site at http://osos.boi.go.th/. BOI identifies eligible activities for its investment incentives (detailed below) covering hundreds of types of businesses. Generally, the most generous incentives are offered to those projects that bring new technology to Thailand and those that invest in less developed provinces. These projects are usually referred to by BOI as "priority activities."

There are two basic types of BOI incentives: tax-based (including tax holidays and tariff exemptions) and non-tax privileges (guarantees, special permissions, services, etc.). The minimum investment amount is 1 million baht (approximately $33,000), excluding the cost of land and working capital; however, small and medium industries in certain activities with minimum investment of 500,000 baht (approximately $16,700), excluding the cost of land and working capital, are also eligible for the incentives. Projects with an investment of 10 million Thai baht (approximately US$330,000) or more, excluding the cost of land and working capital, are typically required to obtain international standards certifications, such as International Standards Organization (ISO) 9000. BOI requires investors to submit evidence of compliance with the conditions of their approval in order to claim incentive benefits. BOI previously lifted all local content and export requirements.

Specific BOI incentives include:

- Tax incentives: exemptions or reductions of import duties on imported machinery; reductions of import duties on imported raw materials and components; exemptions from corporate income taxes for three to eight years; and, deductions from net income of infrastructure costs.
- Permissions: to bring in foreign nationals to undertake investment feasibility studies; to bring in foreign technicians and experts to work under promoted projects; to own land for carrying out promoted activities.
- Guarantees: against nationalization; against competition by new state enterprises; against state monopolization of the sale of products similar to those produced by promoted firms; against price controls; against tax-exempt import by government agencies or state enterprises of competitive products; and, of permission to export.

Tax incentives offer the greatest advantages, though their relative value has declined in recent years with the general reduction of import duties and elimination of the former business tax system. The Value Added Tax (VAT) Law, which eliminated the business tax exemption, has no provision for BOI to offer VAT exemptions or reductions. Investors must submit an application form along with supporting documentation to be considered for incentives. In most cases, BOI decides within 40-60 working days whether or not a project is eligible for investment privileges. BOI typically completes its review of applications for projects valued in excess of 750 million baht (approximately US$24 million) within 90 working days.

The maximum allowable debt-to-equity ratio is 3:1 for a newly established project, but expansion projects are considered on a case-by-case basis. With the exception of electronic and agricultural investments, regardless of overall investment size, projects must produce added value equal to at least 20 percent of sales revenue. For projects with investment capital more than 80 million baht (about US$2.7 million), excluding land and working capital, a feasibility study must be presented at the time of application. Adequate environmental protection systems must be installed for projects with a potential environmental threat.

State-enterprise projects are not eligible for BOI promotions, but concession projects (either Build Transfer Operate or Build Operate Transfer) by the private sector are eligible with some restrictions.

BOI's eligible activities for investment privileges are divided into seven categories. These seven categories cover hundreds of actual business activities. The complete list can be found at www.boi.go.th/english/about /eligible_ activities.asp.

- Category 1: Agriculture and agricultural products;
- Category 2: Mining, ceramics and basic metals;
- Category 3: Light industry;
- Category 4: Metal products, machinery and transport equipment;
- Category 5: Electronic industry and electrical appliances;
- Category 6: Chemicals, paper, and plastics;
- Category 7: Services and public utilities.

Each year, BOI also selects certain business activities under the seven categories as priority investment activities. BOI traditionally gives maximum incentive packages to these priority investment activities and sometime regardless of locations. These activities have included agriculture and agro-industries; research and development; public utilities; infrastructure and basic services; biotechnology; alternative energy; manufacture of high technology products; and environmental protection and conservation.

As part of its policy to encourage investment throughout the country, BOI divides the country into three zones: Zone 1 (Bangkok and 5 surrounding provinces), Zone 2 (a grouping of 12 other provinces, mostly in the central region), and Zone 3 (the remaining 59 provinces with low income and less-developed infrastructure). BOI actively encourages investment in Zone 3, which includes the least developed provinces of Thailand, by offering maximum incentive packages. BOI also promotes the relocation of projects from Zone 1 to Zone 2 and Zone 3; however, in order to be eligible for new incentives, these projects must relocate to an industrial estate or a promoted industrial zone. More details are available on BOI's website.

Majority or total foreign ownership is permitted for BOI-approved investment projects in the manufacturing sector; however, for projects in agriculture, animal husbandry, fishery, mineral exploration and mining, and service businesses under Schedule One of the Foreign Business Act of 1999, Thai nationals must hold shares totaling not less than 51 percent of the registered capital.

In an attempt to revive the economies of the three southernmost provinces (Pattani, Yala, and Narathiwat), BOI launched a special package in mid-2007. The package includes maximum tax incentives, including eight-year corporate income tax holidays plus a 50 percent reduction on corporate income tax for the following five years, an exemption of import duties on machinery and raw materials, and deduction of infrastructure construction and installation cost up to 25 percent of capital investment. The applicable period for double deduction of public utilities and transportation costs was extended to 15 years. In 2009, BOI broadened the investment promotion scope to allow all types of eligible activities to apply for the promotion incentives in Pattani, Yala, and Narathiwat. In addition, the deadline for applications was extended to December 2012.

In June 2010, BOI signed a cooperation agreement with the Thai Ministry of Justice's Office of Public Sector Anti-Corruption Commission (PACC) to improve protection for foreign investors and entrepreneurs from corruption. Both agencies will increase information sharing and open new channels to receive complaints from investors affected by corruption by government officials.

In late 2011, severe flooding damaged 1,775 of BOI's existing promoted companies worth a combined investment value of 624 billion baht (about US$21 billion) or roughly 9 percent of the total investment for the past ten years. The BOI issued the following measures to help minimize business disruptions:

- Affected factories are allowed to temporarily relocate elsewhere to continue their production for a period of six months with a possible extension period from the application submission date;
- Manufacturing processes can be allowed to be outsourced partially or wholly;

- Affected companies are allowed to export their machineries to be used for overseas production;
- BOI would cooperate with the Department of Employment and foreign Embassies to facilitate the use of Thai workers from the flood-affected companies at the overseas production facilities;
- BOI, Ministry of Labor and the Immigration Bureau would assist companies to bring in foreign experts and technicians to rehabilitate the factories;
- Duty-free importation of replacement machinery is allowed until the end of June 2012;
- Imported raw materials damaged by the flooding can be counted as part of the waste allowance without any tax burden.

In addition, the BOI organized a CEO Forum in January 2012 during its annual BOI Fair to announce a long-term flood prevention action plan. It is also notable that Yingluck Shinawatra's government announced policy plans to reduce the corporate income tax rate from the current 30 percent to 23 percent from January 2012 and to 20 percent from January 2013 onward.

RIGHT TO PRIVATE OWNERSHIP AND ESTABLISHMENT

Private entities may establish and own business enterprises. The principal forms of business organization under Thai law are sole proprietorships, partnerships, limited companies, and public limited companies. In addition, branches of foreign corporations are recognized, and a "representative" or "liaison" office of a foreign company may receive special recognition. Regardless of the form of business organization, most businesses must apply for business registration. Establishment of a business in certain sectors by a foreign entity may be restricted by the Foreign Business Act. U.S. investors may benefit from the Treaty of Amity and Economic Relations (AER) as discussed above.

A Thai public limited company is similar to a corporation in the United States, and may be wholly owned by a foreigner unless the corporation is involved in a business activity reserved for Thai nationals. A public limited company is allowed to offer its shares to the public. Eight laws pertaining to individual industries limit foreign ownership of companies listed on the Stock Exchange of Thailand.

PROTECTION OF PROPERTY RIGHTS

Property rights are guaranteed by the Constitution against condemnation or nationalization without fair compensation. Secured interests in property are recognized and enforced. Thailand has a civil law system under which all laws are embodied in statutes or codes promulgated by the government. This practice is in contrast to the common law system in many Western countries, where court interpretations of statutes serve as governing legal precedent. There is an independent judiciary that provides a forum for settlement of disputes. Agencies of the government, as parties to commercial contracts, may be sued in the courts, and cannot raise a defense of sovereign immunity. However, state property is not subject to execution. There are four basic codes: Civil and Commercial Code, Criminal Code, Civil Procedure Code, and Criminal Procedure Code. In adopting these codes early in the twentieth century, Thailand selected features of the two major Western legal systems (common law and civil law), and adapted to circumstances in Thailand provisions drawn from Great Britain, Germany, Switzerland, France, Japan, Italy, India, and other foreign systems. Decisions and rulings of the judiciary and civil service can have considerable force as precedents.

There are three levels to the judicial system in Thailand: the Court of First Instance, which handles most matters at inception, the Court of Appeals, and the Supreme Court. There are specialized courts such as the Labor Court, Family Court, Tax Court, the Central Intellectual Property and International Trade Court, and the Bankruptcy Court. Widespread counterfeiting and piracy continue to plague intellectual property rights owners in Thailand. Particular areas of concern include counterfeiting of pharmaceuticals, cosmetics, apparel, and accessories. Piracy rates are also high for motion pictures, music, business and entertainment software. The lack of sustained and coordinated enforcement, and, in particular, the failure to prosecute and penalize high level offenders, remains a substantial problem. The vast majority of criminal IP cases in Thailand are brought against retailers caught with relatively little infringing product. In addition to problems with counterfeiting and piracy, rights holders cite concerns about long delays in the patent process due to the large backlog of unexamined patent applications. Due to these concerns, Thailand has been on the Special 301 Priority Watch List since 2007. The government continues to develop measures to improve protection and enforcement of intellectual property rights.

Thailand amended its legal regime to comply with the WTO Agreement on Trade Related Aspects of Intellectual Property (TRIPs) in the mid-1990s, but questions remain about Thailand's implementation of obligations to protect pharmaceutical and agricultural test data from unfair commercial use, treatment of conflicting trademarks, and geographical indications. Since that time, Thailand has not kept pace with international intellectual property (IP) legal developments, in areas such as broadcasting and digital copyright. Thailand is signatory to long-standing IP agreements such as the Berne and Paris Conventions, but not the World Intellectual Property Organization Copyright Treaty (WCT) or Performances and Phonograms Treaty (WPPT). Thailand acceded to the Patent Cooperation Treaty in 2009.

Transparency of Regulatory System

In 1999, Thailand enacted the Trade Competition Act together with the Price of Merchandises and Services Act to strengthen the government's ability to regulate market monopolies and price fixing. The Trade Competition Act applies to all business activities with the exception of state-owned enterprises, cooperatives, agricultural and cooperative groups, government agencies, and certain enterprises exempted by the law. The law established a Trade Competition Commission with the authority to place limitations on market share and revenues of firms with substantial control of individual market sectors, to block mergers, and other forms of business combinations, and to levy fines for price fixing and other proscribed activities. Since the law's implementation, several foreign motorcycle distributors were found guilty of violating the law by forcing sales agencies to sell only their brands.

The government continues to have the authority to control the price of specific products under the Price of Merchandises and Services Act. The Department of Internal Trade under the Ministry of Commerce administers this law and interacts with the affected companies although only the "Committee on Price of Merchandise and Service" make the final decision on what products to add or remove from price controls. As of October 2011, out of 42 controlled commodities and services, only sugar is subject to a price ceiling. Besides the 42 controlled commodities, practically any producer of consumer products is prohibited from raising prices without first notifying the Committee of its intention to do so. The government also uses its controlling stakes in major suppliers of products and services such as Thai Airways and PTT to influence prices in the market. Thailand has extensive legislation aimed at the protection of the environment, including the National Environmental Quality Act, the Hazardous Substances Act, and the Factories

Act. Food purity and drug efficacy are controlled and regulated by a Food and Drug Administration with authority similar to its U.S. counterpart. Likewise, labor and employment standards are set and administered by the Ministry of Labor.

U.S. businesses have repeatedly expressed concern about the lack of transparency of the Thai customs regime and the significant discretionary authority exercised by Customs Department officials. The U.S. Government and industries also have expressed concern about the inconsistent application of Thailand's transaction valuation methodology and repeated use of arbitrary values by the Customs Department. In August 2009, the Thai government proposed a series of reforms to its customs laws and procedures. Following the change in government in July 2011, amendments to address the penalty regime need to be resubmitted to the Cabinet before they can be sent to Parliament.

Consistent and predictable enforcement of government regulations remains problematic for investment in Thailand. Gratuity payments to civil servants responsible for regulatory oversight and enforcement remain a common practice. Firms that refuse to make such payments can be placed at a competitive disadvantage when compared to other firms in the same field. However, most observers believe that the overall trend toward transparency in regulatory enforcement is positive, especially for foreign-owned businesses.

EFFICIENT CAPITAL MARKETS AND PORTFOLIO INVESTMENT

The Thai government maintains a regulatory framework that broadly encourages investment and largely avoids market-distorting support for specific sectors. Government policies generally do not restrict the free flow of financial resources to support product and factor markets, and credit is generally allocated on market terms rather than by "directed lending." Legal, regulatory, and accounting systems are largely transparent, despite significant problems in some areas. The Thai government has devoted considerable effort to bringing these systems into line with international norms, and important progress has been made. However, there is more to be done to implement the legal and regulatory changes, and the lack of skilled labor will limit overall progress in some areas, particularly auditing, for the foreseeable future.

In 2002, Thailand established the National Corporate Governance Committee (NCGC), chaired by the Prime Minister, to implement international-standard corporate governance policies. Thailand's main equity market is the Stock Exchange of Thailand (SET) and a secondary market for small and medium-sized enterprises are trading on the Market for Alternative Investment (MAI). In 2012, local retail investors accounted for 53.3 percent of total trading volume, foreign investors for 25.2 percent, and proprietary trading for 13.5 percent, and local institutional investors for 8.0 percent. In conjunction with Thai Rating and Information Services Co., Ltd. (TRIS), the Stock Exchange of Thailand (SET) and the Thai Securities and Exchange Commission (SEC) began rating companies on their corporate governance practices. Foreign investors are not restricted from borrowing on the local market, but there are a number of regulations that affect foreign portfolio investment. Thailand maintains regulatory maximum foreign ownership limits, and shares of listed companies are traded on both a domestic and alien (or foreign) board to enable authorities to track foreign ownership.

Limits on foreign ownership of Thai companies are perhaps most prominent in the financial sector. In theory, the private sector has access to a wide variety of credit instruments, ranging from fixed term lending to overdraft protection to bills of exchange and bonds. However, private debt markets are not well-developed, and most corporate financing, whether for short-term working capital needs, trade financing, or project financing, is commercial bank or financial institution borrowing.

The Thai Asset Management Corporation (TAMC), which was established in 2001, is a major component of the government's financial reform plan with broad legal powers to expedite debt restructuring and press creditors and debtors to the negotiating table. Assets are transferred at collateral value, excluding personal guarantee, with payment coming in the form of ten-year non-negotiable bonds issued by TAMC and guaranteed by the Financial Institution Development Fund (FIDF), a financial arm of the Bank of Thailand. Interest paid by the bonds is tied to average deposit rates quoted by Thailand's five largest banks. According to the decree that created TAMC, the corporation would be dissolved in June 2011 with two more years for asset liquidation by June 2013. All remaining assets will be sold to the former institutional transferors (commercial banks, finance companies, private asset management companies) at an agreed price. If the former institutional transferors are not willing to repurchase such assets, TAMC will sell the assets to the other two smaller state asset management companies, Sukhumvit Asset Management and Bangkok Commercial Asset Management.

In addition to legal limits on foreign ownership in certain sectors, Thai firms employ defenses against foreign investment primarily through cross- and stable-shareholding arrangements. Such defenses against hostile takeovers are typically applied against all potential investors, rather than against foreign potential investors alone. Companies are permitted to specify limits on foreign ownership more strict than those established by the government. In general, limits on foreign ownership and participation in the Thai economy have eased since the Asian Financial Crisis.

COMPETITION FROM STATE OWNED ENTERPRISES

State-owned enterprises operate primarily in the utility, energy, telecommunications, banking, tobacco, agriculture and transportation sectors. At the end of 2011, Thailand's 56 state-owned enterprises (SOEs) had revenues of around 4.29 trillion Thai baht (approximately US$140.8 billion), employed approximately 272,568 people (0.7 percent of the Thai labor force), and accounted for approximately 41 percent of Gross Domestic Product (GDP). Of the SOEs' total revenue, around eighty percent comes from the energy sector.

Private enterprises are generally not allowed to compete with state-owned enterprises under the same terms and conditions with respect to access to markets, credit, and other business operations such as licenses and supplies, except in the banking sector. The government announced its intention to allow more private companies to compete with SOEs, in particular in the telecommunications, energy, and transport sectors. The government regularly allocates three to four percent of its annual budget expenditures to fund the SOEs. The government can temporarily provide short-term credit facilities, loan guarantees, or capital injections for troubled SOEs. This assistance usually focuses on those SOEs that have not been corporatized or are operating in loss. Corporate board seats are typically allocated to senior government officials or other politically-affiliated individuals. All SOEs are required by law to submit annual financial reports to the Office of the Auditor General. Publicly-listed state-owned enterprises, such as Thai Airways, are required to publish their financial reports. Currently, there are only 6 SOEs listed in the Stock Exchange of Thailand (SET), including Krung Thai Bank (1989 listed year), THAI Airways (1991), PTT (2001), AOT (2004), MCOT (2004) and PTTEP (1993), accounting for around 18 percent of the SET's total market capitalization. As for procurements, state-owned enterprises, like government agencies, reserve the right to accept or reject any or all bids at any time and may also modify the technical requirements during the bidding process, if, according to regulations, corruption is suspected. The latter provision allows considerable leeway to state-owned enterprises in managing procurements, while denying bidders recourse to challenge procedures. Allegations frequently surface that changes are made in procurements.

Thailand currently does not have a sovereign wealth fund.

Corporate Social Responsibility

There is wide recognition and awareness of the value of corporate social responsibility (CSR) initiatives among Thai producers and consumers, but many companies still lack a full understanding of the generally accepted CSR principles such as the OECD Guidelines for Multinational Enterprises. CSR is most often identified as individual philanthropic projects or community service of companies, rather than as an overall corporate strategy aimed to improve the community in which the companies operate. Companies that pursue CSR are viewed favorably by the public.

Many business associations, including the American Chamber of Commerce, are actively supporting the development of CSR programs in Thailand. Since 2007, the American Chamber of Commerce Corporate Social Responsibility Excellence Awards have encouraged the expansion of CSR programs by identifying best practices of companies in Thailand. Many CSR programs incorporate the Embassy's Thai-U.S. Creative Partnership to work directly with local partner organizations on long-term projects training and promoting opportunities in innovative sectors, especially renewable energy, IT, and microfinance projects. The AMCHAM ACE program also tracks continuous improvement.

Both the Thai Chamber of Commerce (TCC) and the Federation of Thai Industries (FTI) have undertaken several CSR projects over the past years. The Joint Standing Committee on Commerce, Industry, and Banking of Thailand (JSCCIB) has also established a CSR committee that consolidates reports on activities from both TCC and FTI members.

Political Violence

Thailand, following the landslide victory in parliamentary elections July 3, 2011 by the Puea Thai party, has experienced a reprieve from the instability that had hampered the Thai political system since the September 2006 military coup that deposed Prime Minister Thaksin Shinawatra. Throughout the second half of 2008, a political protest group called the People's Alliance for Democracy (PAD) and nicknamed the "yellow shirts," held large demonstrations against the government, notably seizing Bangkok's civilian airports from November 25, 2008 through December 3, 2008.

Protestors sympathetic to former Prime Minister Thaksin Shinawatra, and opposed to PAD and the then-government, also held large rallies in Bangkok. This group of Thaksin supporters, known as the United Front for Democracy against Dictatorship (UDD), aka the "red-shirts," staged demonstrations against Prime Minister Abhisit in early 2009, culminating in the disruption of a major regional Asian summit in Pattaya and riots in the streets of Bangkok in April of 2009. A subsequent protest by the UDD March 12 – May 19, 2010 resulted in 91 deaths and caused an estimated $1.5 billion in arson-related property losses.

Another important political problem for the Thai government is the ongoing political violence in Thailand's southern-most provinces (Yala, Narathiwat, and Pattani). Efforts to quell the ethno-nationalist insurgency, which has led to over 4,000 deaths since 2004, have not yet had much effect.

Thailand and Cambodia have disputed sections of their historic boundary which resulted in sporadic border clashes between 2008-11. Most significantly, both claim the grounds around the Preah Vihear temple, although the temple itself was awarded to Cambodia in a 1962 ICJ ruling. Cambodia has requested that the ICJ clarify its ruling to include ownership of the disputed grounds, and both countries are awaiting a possible decision in 2013. Thai-Cambodian tensions have subsided over the last year and both governments meet regularly to discuss border issues, though tensions could rise again when the ICJ delivers its verdict in late 2013.

CORRUPTION

Thailand has several laws to combat corruption. The independent National Anti- Corruption Commission (NACC) together with the Public Anti-Corruption Commission (PACC), coordinate official efforts against corruption and hold broad investigatory authority. In addition to these two agencies, the Office of the Ombudsman, the Constitutional Court, the Election Commission, the Office of the Auditor General, and the Human Rights Commission have anti-corruption responsibilities. In December 2003, Thailand became a signatory to the U.N. Convention Against Corruption ratifying the convention in March 2011. In April 2005, Thailand endorsed the ADB-OECD Anticorruption Action Plan for Asia and the Pacific, and assigned the Ministry of Justice to implement the Action Plan. The Office of Public Sector Anti-Corruption Commission, under the Ministry of Justice, was established to assist the NACC by investigating cases of lower ranking government officials.

According to some studies, a cultural propensity to forgive bribes as a normal part of doing business and to equate cash payments with finders' fees or consultants' charges, coupled with the low salaries of civil servants, encourages officials to accept illegal inducements. American executives with experience in Thailand often advise new-to market companies that it is far easier to avoid corrupt transactions from the beginning than to stop such practices once a company has been identified as willing to operate in this fashion. American firms that comply with the strict guidelines of the Foreign Corrupt Practices Act are able to compete successfully in Thailand.

Recent Thai administrations have stated publicly their intention to improve transparency in the evaluation of bids and the awarding of contracts. Despite recent improvements, both foreign and Thai companies continue to complain about irregularities in the Thai Customs Department. Increasing media scrutiny of public figures has raised political pressure to curtail favoritism and corruption. However, convictions against public officials on corruption-related charges are rare, and the legal system offers inadequate deterrence against corruption.

The press features frequent allegations of irregularities in public contracts, most notably over the use of public lands, procurement favoritism (e.g., revising requirements so that a preferred company wins over its competitors), and police complicity in a variety of illegal activities. In January 2010, the Thai press widely reported news of the U.S. Department of Justice indictment of a former Thai tourism minister accused of taking bribes from an American couple seeking to do business in Bangkok. In November 2011, the Permanent Secretary in the Ministry of Transportation resigned over allegations of corruption and bribery after large sums of cash were discovered in his home allegedly from transportation contract kickbacks. In 2012 the Deputy Prime Minister and Interior Minister resigned after it was determined that he was involved in an improper land deal.

Corruption, including bribery, raises the costs and risks of doing business. Corruption has a corrosive impact on both market opportunities overseas for U.S. companies and the broader business climate. It also deters international investment, stifles economic growth and development, distorts prices, and undermines the rule of law. It is important for U.S. companies, irrespective of their size, to assess the business climate in the relevant market in which they will be operating or investing, and to have an effective compliance program or measures to prevent and detect corruption, including foreign bribery. U.S. individuals and firms operating or investing in foreign markets should take the time to become familiar with the relevant anticorruption laws of both the foreign country and the United States in order to properly comply with them, and where appropriate, they should seek the advice of legal counsel.

The U.S. Government seeks to level the global playing field for U.S. businesses by encouraging other countries to take steps to criminalize their own companies' acts of corruption, including bribery of foreign public officials, by requiring them to uphold their obligations under relevant international conventions. A U. S. firm that believes a competitor is seeking to use bribery of a foreign public official to secure a contract should bring this to the attention of appropriate U.S. agencies, as noted below.

U.S. Foreign Corrupt Practices Act

In 1977, the United States enacted the Foreign Corrupt Practices Act (FCPA), which makes it unlawful for a U.S. person, and certain foreign issuers of securities, to make a corrupt payment to foreign public officials for the purpose of obtaining or retaining business for or with, or directing business to, any person. The FCPA also applies to foreign firms and persons who take any act in furtherance of such a corrupt payment while in the United States.

The U.S. Department of Justice (DOJ) and the Securities and Exchange Commission released a Resource Guide to the U.S. Foreign Corrupt Practices Act. The Guide is an excellent resource on the FCPA for U.S. companies with questions about the statute and its enforcement. The Guide explains the statute in detail and contains hypothetical, examples of actual enforcement actions, and summaries of FCPA case law and DOJ opinion releases. For this and other useful resources visit the DOJ Webpage: http://www.justice.gov/criminal/fraud/fcpa/guidance/.

Guidance on the U.S. FCPA

The Department of Justice's (DOJ) FCPA Opinion Procedure enables U.S. firms and individuals to request a statement of the Justice Department's present enforcement intentions under the anti-bribery provisions of the FCPA regarding any proposed business conduct. The details of the opinion procedure are available on DOJ's Fraud Section Website at www.justice.gov/criminal/fraud/fcpa. Although the Department of Commerce has no enforcement role with respect to the FCPA, it supplies general guidance to U.S. exporters who have questions about the FCPA and about international developments concerning the FCPA. For further information on the FCPA, transparency and anti-bribery initiatives, see the Office of the Chief Counsel for International Counsel, U.S. Department of Commerce, website, at http://www.commerce.gov/os/ogc/transparency-and-anti-bribery-initiatives.

More general information on the FCPA is available at the Websites listed below. Exporters and investors should be aware that generally all countries prohibit the bribery of their public officials, and prohibit their officials from soliciting bribes under domestic laws. Most countries are required to criminalize such bribery and other acts of corruption by virtue of being parties to various international conventions discussed above.

Other Instruments

It is U.S. Government policy to promote good governance, including host country implementation and enforcement of anti-corruption laws and policies pursuant to their obligations under international agreements. Since enactment of the FCPA, the United States has been instrumental to the expansion of the international framework to fight corruption. Several significant components of this framework are the OECD Convention on Combating Bribery of Foreign Public Officials in International Business Transactions (OECD Anti-bribery Convention), the United Nations Convention against Corruption (UN Convention), the Inter-American Convention against Corruption (OAS Convention), the Council of Europe Criminal and Civil Law Conventions, and a growing list of U.S. free trade agreements. Thailand is party to the UN Anticorruption Convention; Thailand is also a member of the Asia/Pacific Group against Money Laundering (APG).

OECD Anti-bribery Convention: Thailand is not a party to the OECD Convention (see http://www.oecd.org/dataoecd/59/13/40272933.pdf).

UN Convention: Thailand is a party to the UN Convention (see http://www.unodc.org/unodc/en/treaties/CAC/signatories.html).

OAS Convention: Thailand is not a party to the OAS Convention (see http://www.oas.org/juridico/english/Sigs/b-58.html).

Council of Europe Criminal Law and Civil Law Conventions: Thailand is not a member of the Council of Europe Conventions (see www.coe.int/greco).

Free Trade Agreements: The United States does not have an FTA with Thailand (for U.S. FTAs see U.S. Trade Representative Website: http://www.ustr.gov/trade-agreements/free-trade-agreements).

Local Laws: U.S. firms should familiarize themselves with local anticorruption laws, and, where appropriate, seek legal counsel. While the U.S. Department of Commerce cannot provide legal advice on local laws, the Department's U.S. and Foreign Commercial Service can provide assistance with navigating the host country's legal system and obtaining a list of local legal counsel.

Assistance for U.S. Businesses: The U.S. Department of Commerce offers several services to aid U.S. businesses seeking to address business-related corruption issues. For example, the U.S. and Foreign Commercial Service can provide services that may assist U.S. companies in conducting their due diligence as part of the company's overarching compliance program when choosing business partners or agents overseas. The U.S. Foreign and Commercial Service can be reached directly through its offices in every major U.S. and foreign city, or through its Website at www.trade.gov/cs. The Departments of Commerce and State provide worldwide support for qualified U.S. companies bidding on foreign government contracts through the Commerce Department's Advocacy Center and State's Office of Commercial and Business Affairs. Problems, including alleged corruption by foreign governments or competitors, encountered by U.S. companies in seeking such foreign business opportunities can be brought to the attention of appropriate U.S. government officials, including local embassy personnel and through the Department of Commerce Trade Compliance Center "Report a Trade Barrier" Website at http://www.tcc.export.gov/Report_a_Barrier/index.asp.

Anti-Corruption Resources: Some useful resources for individuals and companies regarding combating corruption in global markets include the following:

- Information about the U.S. Foreign Corrupt Practices Act (FCPA), including a "Lay- Person's Guide to the FCPA" is available at the U.S. Department of Justice's Website at: http://www.justice.gov /criminal/fraud/fcpa/guidance/.
- Information about the OECD Anti-bribery Convention including links to national implementing legislation and country monitoring reports is available at: http://www.oecd.org/department/0,3355,en_2649_ 3485

9_1_1_1_1_1,00.html. See also new Anti-bribery Recommendation and Good Practice Guidance Annex for companies: http://www.oecd.org/dataoecd/11/40/44176910.pdf

- General information about anticorruption initiatives, such as the OECD Convention and the FCPA, including translations of the statute into several languages, is available at the Department of Commerce Office of the Chief Counsel for International Commerce Website: http://www.ogc.doc.gov/trans_anti_bribery.html.
- Transparency International (TI) publishes an annual Corruption Perceptions Index (CPI). The CPI measures the perceived level of public-sector corruption in 180 countries and territories around the world. The CPI is available at: http://cpi.transparency.org/cpi2012. TI also publishes an annual Global Corruption Report which provides a systematic evaluation of the state of corruption around the world. It includes an in-depth analysis of a focal theme, a series of country reports that document major corruption related events and developments from all continents and an overview of the latest research findings on anti-corruption diagnostics and tools. See http://www.transparency.org/publications/gcr.
- The World Bank Institute publishes Worldwide Governance Indicators (WGI). These indicators assess six dimensions of governance in 212 countries, including Voice and Accountability, Political Stability and Absence of Violence, Government Effectiveness, Regulatory Quality, Rule of Law and Control of Corruption. See http://info.worldbank.org/governance/wgi/sc_country.asp. The World Bank Business Environment and Enterprise Performance Surveys may also be of interest and are available at: http://go.worldbank.org/RQQXYJ6210.
- The World Economic Forum publishes the Global Enabling Trade Report, which presents the rankings of the Enabling Trade Index, and includes an assessment of the transparency of border administration (focused on bribe payments and corruption) and a separate segment on corruption and the regulatory environment. See http://www.weforum.org/en/initiatives/gcp/GlobalEnablingTradeReport/index.htm.
- Additional country information related to corruption can be found in the U.S. State Department's annual Human Rights Report available at http://www.state.gov/g/drl/rls/hrrpt/.

- Global Integrity, a nonprofit organization, publishes its annual Global Integrity Report, which provides indicators for 92 countries with respect to governance and anti-corruption. The report highlights the strengths and weaknesses of national level anti-corruption systems. The report is available at: http://report.globalintegrity.org/.

BILATERAL INVESTMENT AGREEMENTS

The 1966 iteration of the U.S.-Thai Treaty of Amity and Economic Relations (AER), discussed above, allows U.S. citizens and businesses incorporated in the U.S., or in Thailand that are majority-owned by U.S. citizens, to engage in business on the same basis as Thai nationals. Under the AER, Thailand is permitted to apply restrictions to American investment only in the fields of communications, transport, banking, the exploitation of land or other natural resources, and domestic trade in agricultural products.

In October 2002, the U.S. and Thailand signed a bilateral Trade and Investment Framework Agreement (TIFA). The TIFA establishes a Trade and Investment Council (TIC), which serves as a forum for discussion of bilateral trade and investment issues such as intellectual property rights, customs, investment, biotechnology, and other areas of mutual concern.

Thailand also has bilateral investment agreements with 39 countries, including China, India, Taiwan, S. Korea, United Kingdom, and members of the Association of Southeast Asian Nations (ASEAN). These agreements establish guidelines for expropriation compensation and the repatriation of capital, but do not include national treatment provisions.

OPIC AND OTHER INVESTMENT INSURANCE PROGRAMS

The Overseas Private Investment Corporation (OPIC) can provide political risk insurance for inconvertibility and transfer, expropriation, and political violence for U.S. investments including equity, loans and loan guarantees, technical assistance, leases, and consigned inventory or equipment. OPIC Insurance is currently insuring two U.S. organizations involved in humanitarian services and economic development in Thailand and providing financing to a U.S. telecommunications firm. OPIC direct loans and loan guarantees are also available for business investments in Thailand, covering sectors as diverse as tourism, transportation, manufacturing, franchising, power, and others. In October 2011, OPIC approved US$250 million in financing to SunEdison Thailand, a subsidiary of MEMC Electronic Materials Inc. (a U.S.-based technology and solar power development company) to develop a pipeline of 51 solar power plants, generating together 520MW, in Thailand. In addition, OPIC supports seven equity funds that are eligible to invest in projects in Thailand.

OPIC established a special line of credit of up to US$175.75 million to mobilize U.S. private sector investment in the reconstruction of nations devastated by the December 2004 tsunami. The credit line was part of an OPIC Tsunami Reconstruction Finance Initiative intended to help speed the rehabilitation of housing and infrastructure in affected countries, including Thailand. Thailand became a member of the Multilateral Investment Guarantee Agency (MIGA) in October 2000.

OPIC-financed loans of up to US$250 million per project are also available for business investments in Thailand, and cover sectors as diverse as tourism, transportation, manufacturing, franchising, power, and others. In addition, OPIC supports six new private equity funds that are eligible to invest in clean and renewable energy projects in emerging markets worldwide, including Thailand. Through OPIC, U.S. investors have access to political risk insurance, debt financing, and equity.

LABOR

According to the National Statistical Office, the Thai labor force in 2012 reached 39.6 million workers out of a total population of 67.9 million. The official unemployment rate in 2011 averaged 0.7% of the labor force despite widespread flooding in industrial estates in the last quarter of the year, which caused a temporary rise in unemployment figures. Despite the increase in minimum wage by 40% nation-wide as of April 1, 2012, unemployment throughout most of 2012 continued to average around 0.72%. A recent World Bank study did not find evidence of a rise in unemployment correlated to the wage hike; however, underemployment (number of workers who work less than 35 hours per week and seeking to work more) rose by 16.4% year-over-year in the third quarter of 2012, evidence of a tight labor market. In order to adjust to rising labor costs, employers reduce the number of hours for each worker. In January 2013, minimum wages increased to $10 (Bt300) per day nationwide, raising the national average minimum wages by 22.4% from 2012.

According to the World Bank, these increases are significantly higher than previous minimum wage hikes which averaged around 2.5% per annum from 2001-2011 and is projected to have an impact on the operations of small and medium size enterprises outside Bangkok and its municipalities.

As of December 2012, 1.3 million illegal migrant workers from Burma, Cambodia, and Laos went through the nationality verification process and received documentation including a passport, visa and work permit. However, civil society estimated that 1 to 2 million migrant workers are still undocumented, primarily from Burma. While the Thai government stated that the documented migrant workers will be equally protected under the Thai Labor Laws, in practice, there are reports that some migrant workers are still receiving wages lower than Thais and have limited access to workmen's compensation fund and training.

Despite rapid growth in the industrial and service sectors, 38% of the Thai labor force is still employed in the agricultural sector. To meet demand for low skilled labor, Bangkok and industrialized zones in Thailand attract large flows of economic migrants from neighboring countries, particularly from Burma and Cambodia, versus workers in agriculture, especially in the Northeast, where agricultural productivity and investment are lower. The ready availability of labor contributed to the rapid growth of Thailand's industrial, services, and construction sectors. The survey done by the World Bank found that firms report acute shortages for technical skills, especially at the vocational school level as well as language and IT skills and soft skills such as leadership and creativity. This technical skill shortage is attributed in large part to a mismatch between market demands and educational preparation. The problem is likely to be exacerbated as Thailand enters a period of demographic aging, with an expected compound annual growth rate of the working age population at only 0.2% between 2010 and 2020. Thailand's Ministry of Labor forecasts a potential 2012 shortfall of up to 700,000 industrial workers, a figure which could reach as high as 1.1 million by the end of 2013 depending on the country's economic performance. Many multinational firms continue to bring in expatriate professionals because qualified local personnel are not available, even at high salaries. Finding, training, and retaining qualified employees to work in the manufacturing facilities being developed in industrial estates, such as those along the Eastern Seaboard, will continue to be a challenging government priority.

According to Ministry of Labor data for 2011, there are 1,373 labor unions operating in Thailand, 1,329 come from private enterprises and 44 come from state-owned enterprises. There are 557,632 unionized workers (roughly 1.4%

of the labor force over the age of 15), 378,813 of which come from private enterprises and 178,819 of which come from state-owned enterprises. Thai law allows private sector workers to form and join trade unions of their choice without prior authorization, but enforcement of labor laws is inconsistent and Thai labor unions are generally weak. Noncitizen migrant workers, whether registered or illegally present, do not have the right to bargain and collect nor serve as union officials, but registered migrants may be members of unions organized and led by Thai citizens. The law restricts affiliations between state enterprise unions and private sector unions.

The labor relations climate is generally peaceful and formal strikes are infrequent. The Labor Protection Act, enacted in 1998, brought labor practices more in line with International Labor Organization (ILO) standards. The law cut the workweek to a maximum of forty-eight hours, with a limit on overtime of 36 hours per week payable at one and one-half times the hourly rate. Hazardous work may not exceed seven hours per day or forty hours per week. All employees are entitled to a vacation of six workdays per year, in addition to thirteen holidays traditionally observed in Thailand. Under the labor law, the employment of children under the age of fifteen is prohibited, and there are restrictions on the employment of children and youths between the ages of fifteen and eighteen. The Thai government amended the Labor Protection Act in 2008 to help promote standards for contract labor. The Act now requires an employer to provide benefits and welfare without discrimination to the contract laborers. The Act also extended protection for employees against sexual abuse and harassment in the workplace. In 2012, two regulations ("Ministerial Regulation on Domestic Work" and "Hazardous Child Labor Work List") were enacted that increased protection to domestic workers and child laborers. Under the new regulations, children under 15 and 18 are prohibited from working in the field of domestic work and fishing vessels. The new regulation on domestic workers will also give annual leave, holidays, and paid sick leave to domestic workers. However, it still fails to address how other issues will be handled, such as minimum wage, working hours, and maternity leave.

FOREIGN-TRADE ZONES/FREE PORTS

The Industrial Estate Authority of Thailand (IEAT), a state-enterprise under the Ministry of Industry, established the first industrial estates in Thailand, including Laem Chabang Industrial Estate in Chonburi Province (eastern) and Map Ta Phut Industrial Estate in Rayong Province (eastern). The IEAT was established under the IEAT Act B.E. 2522 (1979). Foreign owned firms have the same investment opportunities as Thai entities, but the IEAT Act requires that the IEAT Committee has to consider and approve the amount of space for a foreign owned firm to buy or lease land in industrial estates. In practice, there is no record of disapproval for the requested amount of land. More recently, private developers have become heavily involved in the development of these estates. The IEAT currently operates 9 estates, plus 39 more in conjunction with the private sector in 15 provinces nationwide. Private sector developers operate over 50 industrial estates, most of which have received promotion privileges from the Board of Investment.

In addition, the IEAT established 12 special IEAT Free Zones (renamed from export processing zones or free trade zones), reserved for the location of industries manufacturing for export only, to which businesses may import raw materials and export finished products free of duty (including value added tax). These zones are located within industrial estates, and many have customs facilities to speed processing. The free trade zones are located in Chonburi, Lampun, Pichit, Songkhla, Samut Prakarn, Bangkok (at Lad Krabang), Ayuddhya, and Chachoengsao. In addition to these zones, factories may apply for permission to establish a bonded warehouse within their premises to which raw materials, used exclusively in the production of products for export, may be imported duty free.

FOREIGN DIRECT INVESTMENT STATISTICS

According to the Bank of Thailand, foreign direct investment (FDI) (net inflows from non-banking sector only), totaled US$6.2 billion in 2012 (Jan-Sep), compared with US$7.78 billion in 2011 (full year), and US$9.11 billion in 2010 (full year). In 2011, FDI inflows accounted for around 2.2 percent of GDP. In 2012, the sectors that received large amounts of FDI included wholesale and retail (US$967 million), computers and electronics (US$945 million), real estate (US$727 million), chemicals (US$624 million), vehicles (US$589 million), and financial and insurance (US$543 million) sectors..

Japan was the largest source of (net) FDI in 2012 (Jan-Sep) at US$2.2 billion, followed by the U.S. at US$991.5 million, Hong Kong at US$566.6 million, and Netherlands at US$389.7 million). The Bank of Thailand recently has released accumulative FDI data, indicating the US as the third largest FDI

(US$13.4 billion) into Thailand after Japan (US$46.9bn) and Singapore (US$24.1 billion).

From January to November 2012, the Board of Investment approved 45 investment projects by U.S. firms totaling over US$518 million, including FMC Chemical (Thailand) Limited with an estimated value of US$99 million, Pepsi-Cola (Thai) Trading Limited (US$80 million), Hutchinson Technology Operations (Thailand) Company Limited (US$45 million).

INDEX

#

9/11, 20, 30

A

abuse, 35, 38, 43, 46, 64, 67, 71, 74, 85, 89
access, 3, 13, 17, 18, 26, 27, 30, 39, 40, 41, 42, 44, 46, 47, 55, 56, 61, 63, 67, 69, 72, 73, 76, 89, 96, 125, 126, 135, 136
accommodation(s), 39, 60, 76
accounting, 124, 126
ACL, 108
adaptation, 57
adults, 39, 79
advocacy, 42
Afghanistan, viii, 2, 15, 17, 18, 30
age, 39, 50, 67, 70, 71, 72, 74, 75, 77, 79, 85, 86, 88, 136, 137
agencies, 20, 21, 23, 34, 38, 41, 47, 66, 69, 70, 74, 90, 117, 118, 120, 123, 126, 128, 130
aggression, 11
agricultural sector, 85, 89, 136
agriculture, 64, 86, 87, 88, 117, 119, 120, 126, 136
AIDS, 80
airports, 11, 128
Al Qaeda, 18, 20
alternative energy, 119
animal husbandry, 120
anxiety, 8
Appropriations Act, 10, 17, 19
arbitration, 81, 82, 115
architects, 110
armed forces, 20, 38, 48, 50, 53
arms sales, 25
arrest(s), ix, 14, 15, 20, 21, 26, 33, 34, 38, 42, 43, 44, 45, 49, 50, 51, 53, 59, 62, 66, 75, 102, 116
arson, 42, 50, 58, 128
articulation, 117
ASEAN, 22, 25, 26, 28, 30, 116, 134
Asia, viii, 2, 3, 4, 5, 18, 24, 30, 108, 129, 131
assault, 36, 70, 71
assessment, 24, 117, 133
assets, 67, 109, 113, 125
Association of Southeast Asian Nations, 134
asylum, 26, 27, 39, 45, 59, 60, 61, 62
Attorney General, 43, 57
audit, 124
authoritarianism, 23
authority(s), viii, 16, 27, 33, 34, 35, 38, 39, 40, 41, 42, 44, 45, 48, 50, 52, 53, 55, 56, 57, 58, 60, 61, 62, 63, 64, 66, 70, 71, 73, 78, 81, 82, 89, 90, 100, 101, 113, 116, 117, 123, 124, 125, 128
autonomy, 13

awareness, 38, 71, 80, 84, 127

B

Bahrain, 22
bail, 35, 38, 40, 42, 44, 55, 56, 59, 62, 68
ban, 56, 57, 102
Bangkok, vii, viii, x, 1, 2, 4, 5, 7, 8, 10, 11, 12, 13, 15, 20, 21, 25, 26, 28, 30, 31, 35, 38, 39, 41, 43, 54, 55, 61, 62, 67, 71, 79, 94, 102, 105, 107, 110, 115, 119, 125, 128, 129, 136, 138
bank accounts, x, 106
banking, 107, 108, 126, 134, 138
banking sector, 108, 126, 138
bankruptcy(s), x, 106, 115, 116
banks, 107, 108, 109, 112, 113, 125
bargaining, 83, 84
barriers, 41, 107, 117
barter, 19
base, x, 12, 17, 106
basic services, 63, 119
Beijing, viii, 2, 4, 24, 25
belief systems, 95
beneficiaries, 62
benefits, viii, 2, 72, 77, 79, 83, 84, 87, 89, 90, 96, 100, 106, 118, 137
Bilateral, 19, 24, 31, 134
biotechnology, 119, 134
births, 72, 73
blame, 35, 69
blood, 80
bonds, 125
bonuses, 83
Border Patrol, 34, 43, 49
Botswana, 30
brass, vii, 2
bribes, 60, 84, 129, 131
broadcast media, 52, 53, 54, 55
brutality, 38
Buddhism, 52, 94, 95, 98, 99
bureaucracy, 7
bureaucratic elite, 6
Burma, viii, 2, 17, 20, 21, 24, 25, 26, 27, 28, 58, 60, 61, 62, 63, 66, 85, 86, 89, 90, 136
business partners, 132
businesses, 60, 73, 80, 84, 88, 106, 110, 111, 116, 117, 120, 121, 124, 130, 132, 134, 138

C

Cabinet, 110, 124
cabinet members, 9
Cambodia, 4, 6, 13, 25, 27, 28, 30, 58, 63, 85, 86, 89, 94, 102, 128, 136
campaigns, 51, 80
capital adequacy, 108
capital inflow, 111
capital outflow, 114
case law, 130
cash, 129
censorship, 40, 54, 55, 56
central bank, 107
certificate, 64, 107, 110
certification, 97
challenges, 3, 103
Chamber of Commerce, 127
chat rooms, 55
chemical(s), 85, 88, 138
child abuse, 74
child labor, ix, 34, 75, 86, 87, 137
child pornography, 75
children, ix, 24, 34, 39, 40, 46, 50, 62, 63, 64, 67, 71, 72, 73, 74, 75, 77, 84, 85, 86, 87, 88, 97, 137
Chile, 22
China, viii, 2, 4, 22, 24, 25, 30, 31, 94, 102, 108, 134
Christians, 95
CIA, 18, 20, 30
city(s), vii, 1, 35, 55
citizens, 38, 52, 59, 64, 78, 79, 90, 99, 101, 106, 110, 111, 134
citizenship, 63, 64, 73, 78
civil law, 107, 122
civil servants, 80, 82, 124, 129
civil service, 66, 72, 73, 79, 122
civil society, 41, 52, 67, 69, 136
civil war, 77

classes, 100
cleaning, 39
clients, 44, 47
climate, vii, x, 106, 129, 137
clinical assessment, 41
closure, 57, 73
clothing, 21
CNS, 10
coal, 68
coalition government, viii, 10, 33
coercion, 72
Cold War, 3, 17, 30
collaboration, 67
collateral, 125
collective bargaining, 81, 83, 84
commerce, 131
commercial, 24, 53, 54, 79, 86, 108, 112, 114, 115, 122, 123, 125
commercial bank, 108, 112, 114, 125
common law, 122
community(s), ix, 7, 26, 48, 54, 61, 63, 71, 74, 76, 80, 90, 93, 94, 98, 102, 103, 127
community service, 54, 74, 127
compatibility, 97
compensation, 36, 38, 47, 49, 81, 90, 97, 98, 114, 115, 122, 134, 136
competition, viii, 2, 4, 24, 118
competitiveness, 108
competitors, 19, 129, 132
complexity, 64
compliance, 24, 76, 118, 130, 132
compounds, 5
computer, 21, 52, 55, 56
conciliation, 81, 115
confessions, 38, 44
confinement, 40
conflict, ix, 7, 8, 13, 16, 35, 45, 48, 93, 100, 101
confrontation, 7
Congress, vii, 1, 11, 22, 26
consent, 50, 56, 74
conservation, 119
consolidation, 108
Constitution, 95, 122
construction, 88, 89, 120, 136
consumers, 127
controversial, 23, 48, 111
convention, 129
conviction, 4, 38, 53, 55
cooperation, viii, 2, 3, 6, 17, 18, 20, 21, 25, 38, 120
coordination, 14, 15, 20, 63, 67
copyright, 123
corporate governance, 125
corporate restructuring, 116
Corporate Social Responsibility, 127
corporate tax rate, xi, 106
corruption, 3, 4, 7, 9, 11, 43, 46, 66, 67, 78, 120, 127, 128, 129, 130, 131, 132, 133, 134
cosmetics, 122
cost, 20, 46, 87, 108, 118, 120
cost of living, 87
cotton, 21
Council of Europe, 131, 132
Council of Ministers, 110
counsel, 42, 44, 46, 130, 132
counseling, 71
counterfeiting, 122
counterterrorism, 11
Coup, 10, 17, 23
court approval, 71
Court of Appeals, 122
covering, 54, 117, 134
CPI, 133
creativity, 136
creditors, x, 106, 115, 125
creep, 23
crimes, 42, 71, 79
criminal activity, 42
criminal investigations, 55
criminals, 41
crises, x, 5, 106
criticism, 5, 10, 23, 27, 47, 55
cronyism, 23
crowds, 12
crown, 46
cultural norms, 86
culture, 100
currency, x, 106, 113, 114

curriculum, 63, 96

D

damages, 47
danger, 16, 26
Darfur, 18
data collection, 50, 75
DEA, 21
deaths, 12, 18, 23, 35, 39, 44, 58, 89, 128
debtors, 115, 125
deduction, 120
defamation, 38, 55, 56, 95
defendants, 35, 36, 44, 46, 47, 74, 97
deficit, 21
delegates, 48
democracy, vii, 1, 3, 6, 10, 22, 23, 103
Democrat, 6, 11, 13, 35, 55, 111
Democratic Party, 10
demonstrations, vii, 1, 3, 6, 9, 12, 22, 128
denial, 97
Department of Commerce, 22, 131, 132, 133
Department of Defense, 18, 30
Department of Homeland Security, 21
Department of Justice, 129, 130, 132
Department of Labor, 81, 83, 86, 87, 88, 89
deposit accounts, 114
depth, 81, 96, 133
detainees, ix, 33, 39, 40, 41, 42, 43, 44, 47, 59, 66
detention, ix, 33, 38, 39, 40, 41, 42, 45, 49, 59, 60, 61, 62
deterrence, 129
detoxification, 41
dialogues, 5
direct investment, x, 105, 114
directors, 109
disability, 70, 77
disclosure, 52, 67
discrimination, ix, 33, 70, 72, 76, 77, 78, 79, 84, 95, 101, 137
diseases, 39, 88
displaced persons, 60, 63
displacement, 60
disposition, 71
dissidents, 26
distribution, 54, 75, 117
district courts, 45
diversity, 102
DNA, 51
doctors, 89
DOJ, 130
domestic demand, x, 106
domestic laws, 131
domestic violence, 71
dominance, 6
donations, 99
draft, 69, 112
drawing, 8
drinking water, 84
drug addict, 41
drug dependence, 41
drug trafficking, 66, 78
drugs, 23, 35, 41
due process, 41, 114
durability, 3
duty free, 138

E

earnings, 90
East Asia, 16, 18
economic development, x, 14, 105, 134
economic growth, 129
economic integration, 28
economic migrants, 136
economic performance, 136
economic policy, 10
economic reform, x, 106
editors, 23
education, 51, 61, 63, 64, 76, 78, 96, 99
educational exchanges, ix, 94
educational institutions, 79, 96, 98
educational process, 73
election, 5, 6, 9, 10, 12, 65
e-mail, 55
embassy, 8, 102, 103, 132
emergency, 71
emerging markets, 135

emigration, 59
employees, 80, 81, 83, 84, 88, 110, 136, 137
employers, 72, 77, 80, 81, 82, 83, 84, 85, 87, 88, 90, 135
employment, x, 51, 76, 79, 80, 81, 85, 105, 124, 137
employment opportunities, 79
energy, 5, 126
enforcement, 22, 69, 70, 75, 76, 86, 87, 89, 90, 107, 115, 122, 124, 130, 131, 137
England, 108
entrepreneurs, 120
environment, 15, 123, 133
environmental degradation, 78
environmental impact, 117
environmental protection, 25, 119
equipment, 17, 19, 25, 84, 85, 116, 119, 134
equity, 109, 119, 125, 134, 135
equity market, 125
ethnic groups, 27
ethnic minority, 68
ethnicity, ix, 63, 93, 101
EU, 22
Europe, 132
European Union, 22
evidence, 15, 24, 41, 45, 47, 63, 74, 113, 118, 135
examinations, 76
exchange rate, 115
execution, 116, 122
executive branch, 6
exercise, 6, 20, 39, 41, 50
exile, vii, 1, 3, 11
expenditures, 126
expertise, 83
exploitation, ix, 24, 34, 75, 86, 107, 134
export market, viii, 2, 22
exporters, 113, 131
exports, 21, 25
exposure, 56, 85
expulsion, 61, 62
extradition, 21

F

Facebook, 56
factor market, 124
factories, 24, 80, 82, 85, 86, 87, 89, 120, 121, 138
families, 25, 46, 49, 75
family members, 42, 44, 62, 71, 113
FDI, 138
FDI inflow, 138
fear, 54, 75
Federal Bureau of Investigation, 21
films, 57
financial, 9, 15, 107, 109, 113, 114, 115, 116, 117, 124, 125, 126, 138
financial crisis, 9, 109, 116
financial institutions, 107, 113, 114
financial reports, 126
financial resources, 124
financial sector, 125
financial support, 15
fingerprints, 51
fishing, 85, 86, 87, 137
flexibility, 90
flooding, x, 60, 86, 105, 109, 120, 121, 135
floods, x, 106, 109
FMC, 139
food, 39, 60, 61
Food and Drug Administration, 124
force, ix, 8, 16, 17, 18, 33, 34, 35, 38, 47, 66, 122, 135
foreclosure, x, 106, 116
foreign aid, 17
foreign banks, 107, 108
foreign direct investment, x, 21, 105, 138
foreign exchange, 112, 114
foreign firms, 130
foreign investment, x, 106, 107, 125
foreign language, 96
foreign nationals, 118
foreign policy, 4, 5, 13, 26, 28
formal sector, 87
formation, 10
France, 31, 122
fraud, 65, 130, 131, 132

free trade, 131, 138
freedom, vii, ix, 22, 23, 24, 33, 47, 52, 53, 56, 58, 59, 60, 62, 82, 83, 93, 94, 95, 97, 102
friction, 24
funding, 68
funds, 11, 19, 90, 99, 112, 113, 114, 135

G

gambling, 55, 56
garment industry, 86
GATS, 117
gay men, 79
GDP, x, 105, 109, 126, 138
gender identity, 70, 79
General Agreement on Trade in Services, 117
general election, 5
Germany, 122
global markets, 132
goods and services, 114
governance, 7, 8, 11, 15, 117, 125, 131, 133, 134
government budget, 98
governments, viii, 2, 3, 6, 10, 12, 13, 15, 22, 27, 128, 132
governor, 60
grades, 97, 100
Great Britain, 122
Gross Domestic Product, 126
grouping, 16, 119
growth, x, 13, 22, 25, 105, 136
growth rate, 136
guardian, 87
guidance, 117, 130, 131, 132
guidelines, 129, 134
guilt, 46
guilty, 57, 123

H

harassment, 68, 72, 79, 137
harmful effects, 79
harmony, 95, 100
health, viii, 2, 4, 7, 8, 41, 61, 64, 72, 76, 78, 86, 88, 89, 99
health care, 7, 61, 64, 76, 78, 99
health services, 41
hedging, 114
higher education, 96, 99
hiring, 72, 77
history, 6, 12, 14, 25, 30
HIV, 41, 71, 80
HIV/AIDS, 71, 80
Hmong, 27, 39, 61
homes, 71, 86
Hong Kong, 138
host, 6, 27, 60, 131, 132
hostilities, ix, 34
hotel(s), 79, 87, 88, 101
hotspots, 55
House, 65, 69, 102
House of Representatives, 65
household income, 76
housing, 61, 135
hub, viii, 2, 17
human, viii, ix, 2, 9, 22, 24, 26, 33, 37, 38, 39, 40, 41, 44, 46, 47, 50, 52, 57, 67, 68, 69, 75, 101, 103
human right(s), viii, ix, 2, 9, 22, 26, 33, 37, 38, 39, 40, 41, 44, 46, 47, 50, 52, 57, 67, 68, 69, 101, 103
humanitarian organizations, 27, 59
Hungary, 30

I

ideals, 22
identification, 61, 79
identity, ix, 59, 79, 93, 101
image, vii, 1
IMF, x, 9, 106
immigrants, 77, 94
immigration, 27, 39, 89
immunity, 37, 42, 48, 122
imports, 21
imprisonment, 35, 38, 40, 47, 52, 54, 55, 56, 70, 71, 72, 74, 75, 83, 87, 88, 95

improvements, 22, 90, 116, 129
incidence, 43, 88
income, 3, 67, 118, 119, 120, 121
income tax, 118, 120, 121
India, 22, 122, 134
individuals, 23, 35, 36, 37, 38, 41, 42, 44, 45, 48, 49, 51, 58, 63, 72, 73, 79, 80, 81, 86, 114, 126, 130, 132
Indonesia, 5, 20, 28, 94
industry(s), 24, 72, 82, 84, 86, 87, 88, 118, 119, 121, 124, 138
inefficiency, 78
informal sector, 85, 86, 87, 89
information sharing, 120
infrastructure, 28, 118, 119, 120, 135
injections, 126
injuries, 43, 88, 89
injury, 70, 89
inspections, 82, 86, 90
inspectors, 82, 86, 88, 90
institutions, 5, 6, 8, 23, 54, 99, 110, 114
insurgency, ix, 13, 15, 16, 17, 28, 33, 34, 128
integrated circuits, 21
integration, 22, 26
intellectual property, 22, 66, 117, 122, 123, 134
intellectual property rights, 22, 66, 122, 134
intelligence, 14, 15, 20
interest rates, 90
interference, 67, 100
Internal Revenue Service, 21
internally displaced, 59
International Criminal Court, 22
international investment, 129
International Monetary Fund, x, 9, 106
international standards, 86, 118
interrogations, 44
intersex, 79
intervention, 22
intimidation, 26, 38, 55, 65, 68, 102
investment(s), vii, x, 3, 21, 22, 25, 105, 106, 111, 112, 113, 117, 118, 119, 120, 124, 134, 135, 136, 138, 139
investment capital, 119
investment incentive, 117
investment size, 119
investors, x, xi, 10, 25, 105, 106, 107, 110, 112, 117, 118, 120, 121, 125, 126, 131, 135
Iraq, viii, 2, 17, 18
Islam, 16, 94, 103
Israel, 91
issues, viii, 2, 3, 102, 117, 128, 132, 134, 137
Italy, 122
iteration, 106, 134

J

Japan, 6, 16, 20, 22, 122, 138
joint ventures, 107
journalism, 55
journalists, 9, 23, 35, 54
judicial branch, 6, 23
judiciary, 46, 47, 65, 115, 122
jurisdiction, 34, 42, 45, 97, 115
juveniles, 39, 49

K

kill, 55
Korea, 134

L

labor force, 82, 126, 135, 136, 137
labor market, 135
labor relations, 82, 137
landscape, 4
language barrier, 73, 82
language skills, 103
languages, 82, 90, 133
Laos, 6, 17, 25, 27, 28, 58, 63, 85, 86, 89, 136
law enforcement, 15, 21, 41, 71, 81
laws, ix, x, 8, 10, 22, 23, 38, 47, 50, 52, 53, 64, 67, 74, 75, 77, 78, 79, 85, 86, 88, 93,

95, 106, 121, 122, 124, 128, 130, 131, 132, 137
laws and regulations, 64, 67, 77
lawyers, 44, 47, 110
lead, 60
leadership, viii, 2, 3, 5, 7, 14, 15, 20, 26, 28, 103, 136
legislation, 27, 78, 117, 123, 132
lending, 109, 114, 124, 125
liberalization, 117
liberty, 95
light, 88
limited company, 121
limited liability, 109
loan guarantees, 126, 134
loans, 13, 67, 77, 90, 108, 109, 112, 113, 115, 134, 135
local authorities, 41, 60
logistics, 17
loyalty, 8

M

machinery, 88, 118, 119, 120, 121
magnet, 27
MAI, 125
majority, viii, ix, 2, 12, 13, 28, 34, 48, 53, 88, 94, 106, 107, 112, 122, 134
Malaysia, 15, 20, 25, 28, 31, 107
malfeasance, 66, 67
man, 64
management, x, 89, 105, 125
manufacturing, 28, 84, 88, 120, 135, 136, 138
market access, 107, 117
market capitalization, 126
market share, 123
marriage, 64, 74
martial law, ix, 10, 14, 15, 34, 42, 43, 45, 48, 49, 50, 84
mass, 8, 15, 46
materials, 6, 52, 85, 98, 138
matter, 43
media, 7, 23, 52, 54, 55, 71, 129
mediation, 71
medical, 18, 39, 41, 51, 60, 63, 72, 76, 78, 89
medical care, 39
membership, 62
mergers, 123
messages, 40
metals, 119
methodology, 124
Mexico, 30
microorganisms, 85
middle class, 7, 9
Middle East, 17
migrant population(s), 75
migrants, 24, 26, 59, 61, 62, 63, 68, 75, 76, 80, 82, 85, 86, 89, 90, 137
militarization, 98
military, vii, viii, 1, 2, 3, 4, 5, 6, 7, 8, 10, 11, 12, 14, 15, 17, 18, 19, 20, 21, 22, 23, 25, 26, 27, 34, 35, 38, 39, 41, 43, 44, 45, 46, 48, 49, 50, 51, 58, 65, 69, 73, 79, 97, 98, 101, 102, 128
military aid, 17
military dictatorship, 6
military exercises, 6, 17, 20
military government, 10, 11, 14
military school, 50
military-to-military, 3
militia, 50
militias, 26
minimum wage(s), xi, 13, 84, 85, 87, 106, 135, 137
Ministry of Education, 51, 63, 96, 97, 102
minorities, ix, 24, 27, 34, 60, 63, 65, 72
minority groups, 59
minors, 40, 75
mission(s), 17, 18, 110
misuse, 44
momentum, 9
monks, 14, 51, 98, 99, 102
monopoly, 59
Multilateral, 135
multinational firms, 136
murder, 35, 36, 40, 66
music, 122

Muslims, 14, 15, 28, 49, 51, 65, 94, 95, 98, 101, 103
Myanmar, 21

N

narcotics, 9, 20, 21, 26
National Defense Authorization Act, 11
national emergency, 84
national security, 20, 43, 46, 52, 53, 54, 57, 81
nationalism, ix, 7, 93, 101
nationality, 60, 62, 64, 89, 90, 107, 136
natural gas, 26
natural resources, 107, 134
negotiating, 115, 125
negotiation, 82
Netherlands, 138
neutral, 18, 41
New Zealand, 22
NGOs, 38, 45, 47, 49, 50, 51, 58, 61, 62, 63, 67, 68, 70, 72, 73, 75, 79, 80, 87, 90, 94, 98
noncitizens, 64
North Atlantic Treaty Organization (NATO), viii, 2, 17, 19, 30
North Korea, 27, 61
nuisance, 97
nursing, 73

O

OAS, 131
Obama, viii, 2, 4, 5, 26
Obama Administration, viii, 2, 4, 5, 26
OECD, 127, 129, 131, 132, 133
offenders, 39, 40, 71, 74, 122
Office of the Inspector General, 43
oil, 21
online media, 52
open economy, 108
Operation Enduring Freedom, 18
operations, viii, 2, 6, 11, 17, 18, 38, 44, 48, 86, 117, 126, 136
opportunities, 18, 20, 22, 26, 85, 117, 127, 129, 132, 138
opportunity costs, 5
organize, 81, 82, 83
outreach, 41, 80
Overseas Private Investment Corporation, 134
oversight, 55
overtime, 84, 85, 88, 137
ownership, x, 106, 107, 109, 111, 117, 120, 121, 125, 128

P

Pacific, viii, 2, 3, 4, 18, 21, 129, 131
Pakistan, 18
palm oil, 68
parental consent, 74
parents, 64, 75, 76, 89
Parliament, vii, 2, 5, 115, 124
participants, 7, 100
pathologist, 44
peace, 11, 16, 18, 52, 59
peacekeeping, 11, 18
penalties, 3, 40, 43, 52, 53, 56, 66, 70, 71, 74, 75, 83, 107
Pentagon, 18
permission, 44, 58, 59, 60, 74, 85, 111, 113, 117, 118, 138
permit, 39, 79, 89, 90, 108, 109, 110, 136
perpetrators, 71
Persian Gulf, 16
Persian Gulf War, 16
persons with disabilities, ix, 34, 76, 77, 98
Peru, 22
Petroleum, 111
pharmaceutical(s), 122, 123
Philippines, viii, 2, 5, 16, 25, 28
photographs, 51
physical abuse, 38, 41, 63, 71, 74
pipeline, 135
piracy, 18, 122
plastics, 119
platform, 9
playing, 130

PM, 31
police, ix, 8, 14, 15, 33, 34, 35, 37, 38, 39, 40, 41, 42, 43, 44, 45, 46, 47, 48, 51, 52, 53, 57, 60, 66, 70, 71, 79, 80, 89, 97, 129
policy, viii, 2, 13, 26, 67, 78, 79, 89, 90, 107, 112, 119, 121, 131
political affiliations, 69
political crisis, 5
political instability, 5, 13
political opposition, 23
political party(s), vii, 1, 3, 10, 59, 65
political power, 23
political refugees, 27
political system, 3, 22, 23, 128
politics, vii, 1, 6, 7, 8, 9, 10, 11, 65
population, 7, 8, 25, 39, 48, 51, 81, 94, 99, 103, 135, 136
portfolio, 125
portfolio investment, 125
poverty, 64, 87
poverty line, 87
power plants, 135
PRC, 25
precedent(s), 79, 116, 122
preparation, 136
preschool, 77
President, 5, 17, 30
President Obama, 5
presumption of innocence, 46
prevention, 41, 71, 121
price ceiling, 123
principles, 10, 95, 115, 127
prisoners, ix, 33, 39, 40, 41, 43, 46, 47, 66
prisons, 39, 41
private enterprises, 136
private firms, 77
private schools, 99
private sector, 72, 80, 81, 82, 119, 125, 135, 137, 138
private sector investment, 135
privatization, 111
procedural rule, 116
procurement, 11, 129
producers, 127
professionalism, 20
professionals, 136
profit, 109
project, 41, 48, 77, 118, 119, 125, 135
property rights, 122
protection, ix, 33, 35, 47, 52, 59, 61, 62, 70, 74, 80, 98, 101, 115, 120, 122, 123, 125, 137
psychiatrist, 74
psychologist, 74
PTT, 111, 123, 126
public awareness, 75, 86
public education, 100
public figures, 129
public health, 51
public interest, 58
public limited company, 121
public officials, 67, 129, 130, 131
public safety, 52
public schools, 73, 74
public service, 54
public welfare, 59
publishing, 56, 68
punishment, 38, 47, 56, 72, 75, 81, 86
purity, 124

Q

quality of life, 95
questioning, 8
quotas, 100

R

race, 62, 70
radiation, 85
radicals, 15
radio, 52, 53, 54
Ramadan, 101, 102
rape, 70, 74
rating agencies, 109
raw materials, 28, 118, 120, 121, 138
real estate, 67, 114, 138
reception, 102
recidivism, 70

recognition, 64, 121, 127
recommendations, 40, 69, 70
reconciliation, 13, 69, 71
reconstruction, x, 18, 106, 135
recovery, x, 106
recruiting, 50
recurrence, 69
reform(s), x, 6, 10, 13, 26, 106, 124, 125
refugee camps, 60, 61, 62, 63, 64
refugee status, 27, 61, 63
refugees, ix, 26, 27, 31, 33, 39, 41, 59, 60, 61, 62, 63, 64
regionalism, 22
regulations, 40, 41, 45, 58, 72, 77, 80, 85, 88, 89, 90, 107, 114, 116, 124, 125, 127, 137
regulatory bodies, 65
regulatory changes, 124
regulatory framework, 124
regulatory oversight, 124
rehabilitation, 39, 41, 135
rejection, 80
relatives, 23, 90
reliability, viii, 2
relief, viii, 2, 6, 17, 26
religion, 62, 70, 94, 95, 96, 101
religious freedom, vii, ix, 93, 94, 95, 97, 102
remittances, 112, 113
renewable energy, 127, 135
repair, 99
reputation, 27
requirements, 38, 79, 84, 87, 108, 117, 118, 126, 129
resentment, 15
reserves, 110
resettlement, 41, 61, 62, 63
resistance, 25
resources, 15, 47, 69, 76, 90, 130, 132
response, 10, 12, 36, 58, 98
restaurants, 86, 88
restoration, 99
restrictions, x, 11, 55, 59, 78, 79, 106, 107, 109, 112, 117, 119, 134, 137
restructuring, 115, 116, 125
retail, 88, 108, 125, 138
retaliation, 81
revenue, 119
rights, 5, 7, 15, 41, 43, 44, 46, 47, 48, 49, 50, 52, 58, 59, 60, 68, 69, 70, 71, 72, 73, 75, 78, 79, 107, 115, 122
risk(s), 24, 40, 86, 108, 129, 134, 135
risk management, 108
rubber, 21
rule of law, 5, 130
rules, 40, 74, 90, 115, 116
rural areas, 9
rural population, viii, 2

S

safety, 88, 89, 102
sanctions, 26, 82
school, 51, 54, 55, 73, 74, 75, 76, 77, 79, 85, 94, 96, 97, 98, 100, 102, 136
schooling, 63, 73, 96
scope, 120
seafood, 21, 24, 85, 86, 87
security(s), viii, ix, 2, 3, 6, 12, 13, 14, 15, 16, 18, 20, 26, 30, 33, 34, 35, 36, 37, 38, 42, 43, 48, 49, 52, 55, 59, 63, 69, 99, 101, 103, 113, 130
security forces, ix, 12, 13, 14, 15, 33, 34, 35, 36, 37, 48, 49, 63, 69
segregation, 82
seizure, 55, 67
self-interest, 7
Senate, 10, 31, 57, 65, 68, 69
Senate Foreign Relations Committee, 31
sentencing, 45, 70
September 11, 18, 20
service provider, 56
services, 14, 18, 20, 35, 41, 48, 60, 61, 63, 64, 71, 72, 76, 78, 81, 95, 114, 117, 118, 123, 132, 134, 136
sex, ix, 24, 34, 57, 75, 79, 86
sexual abuse, 46, 71, 74, 79, 137
sexual harassment, 66, 72
sexual intercourse, 74, 75
sexual orientation, 70, 79

shelter, 61
shortage, 136
shortfall, 136
shrimp, 85, 86, 87
signals, 54
signs, 36
Singapore, viii, 2, 5, 9, 16, 20, 23, 28, 30, 139
skilled workers, 87
SMS, 40
smuggling, 66, 75, 84
social group, 62
social life, 78
social responsibility, 127
social security, 86, 89
social status, 70
societal abuses, ix, 93, 101
society, 3, 4, 8, 49, 90, 102
software, 122
sole proprietor, 121
Somalia, 18
South Asia, 94
South Korea, 16, 20, 22
Southeast Asia, vii, viii, 1, 2, 3, 4, 6, 16, 17, 18, 20, 24, 25, 27, 28, 30, 134
sovereignty, 13
soybeans, 21
special education, 77
specialization, 110
speculation, 113
speech, ix, 23, 33, 52, 95
Spring, 12
Sri Lanka, 39, 62
stability, 3, 4, 8, 22, 23
staff members, 83
staffing, 69
stasis, 25
state(s), 5, 6, 9, 15, 17, 22, 23, 24, 30, 38, 39, 43, 47, 50, 53, 57, 59, 67, 70, 71, 76, 77, 78, 80, 81, 82, 83, 85, 95, 96, 98, 99, 100, 111, 118, 122, 123, 125, 126, 133, 136, 137
state enterprises, 77, 112, 118
state of emergency, 5
state schools, 77, 100
state-owned enterprises, 83, 123, 126, 136
statistics, 38, 49, 51, 53, 70, 72, 75, 87, 88, 116
statutes, 70, 122
stigma, 80
stimulus, x, 106
stock, 12, 112
stock exchange, 12
strategic cooperation, 25
stress, 15
structure, 112, 117
style, 9, 23, 115
subsistence, 64
succession, 4, 8, 23
Sudan, 18
sugarcane, 86
suicide, 36
supervision, 42, 75, 107
suppliers, 123
suppression, 22
Supreme Court, 43, 45, 65, 66, 67, 82, 83, 97, 116, 122
surveillance, 101
survivors, 70
sustainability, 83
sweat, 85
Switzerland, 122

T

tactics, 21, 38, 116
Taiwan, 134
takeover, 10, 11
tariff, 116, 117, 118
Task Force, 21, 38, 49
tax incentive, 120
tax system, 118
TCC, 127
teachers, 14, 49, 51, 73, 80, 100, 101
technical assistance, 22, 134
technical support, 91
technology, x, 25, 105, 117, 119, 135
technology transfer, x, 105
telecommunications, 9, 23, 81, 117, 126, 134

television stations, 53
tension(s), x, 15, 28, 48, 101, 105, 128
tenure, 13
territorial, 25, 28
territory, 28
terrorism, 18, 28, 58
terrorists, 18, 20
test data, 123
Thaksin, vii, 1, 2, 3, 4, 6, 7, 8, 9, 10, 11, 12, 13, 14, 15, 17, 18, 22, 23, 25, 28, 30, 35, 66, 69, 111, 128
The Foreign Business Act, x, 106
theft, 66
threats, 42, 43, 53
tobacco, 126
torture, 36, 37, 38, 68
total revenue, 126
tourism, ix, 12, 24, 34, 75, 129, 135
tracks, 127
trade, vii, viii, 1, 2, 3, 4, 19, 21, 22, 24, 25, 26, 28, 80, 81, 88, 107, 116, 117, 125, 132, 134, 137, 138
trade agreement, 25
trade deficit, 21
trade union, 80, 81, 137
trademarks, 123
traditions, 102
trafficking, ix, 22, 24, 34, 75
trafficking in persons, ix, 34
training, 11, 18, 20, 44, 49, 50, 71, 75, 77, 83, 127, 136
transactions, 112, 113, 114, 129
transparency, 7, 22, 124, 129, 131, 133
transport, 68, 87, 107, 117, 119, 126, 134
transportation, 76, 81, 120, 126, 129, 135
treaties, 131
treatment, xi, 26, 27, 31, 38, 41, 60, 68, 70, 82, 85, 106, 107, 123, 134
trial, 35, 45, 46, 47, 53, 54, 65, 67, 68, 71
turnout, 10
turnover, 83

U

U.S. assistance, 17
U.S. Department of Commerce, 30, 131, 132
U.S. global military, viii, 2
U.S. policy, 3, 26
U.S. relations, vii, 1
unemployment rate, 135
uniform, xi, 106
unions, 80, 81, 82, 83, 136
United, viii, ix, 2, 3, 4, 5, 6, 7, 10, 16, 17, 19, 20, 21, 22, 24, 25, 26, 27, 28, 42, 94, 102, 108, 110, 115, 121, 128, 130, 131, 132, 134
United Kingdom, 134
United Nations (UN), 10, 17, 22, 27, 28, 37, 38, 41, 50, 52, 58, 61, 68, 72, 75, 78, 110, 115, 131
United Nations High Commissioner for Refugees (UNHCR), 27, 41, 59, 61, 62, 63
United States, viii, ix, 2, 3, 4, 5, 6, 17, 19, 20, 21, 22, 24, 25, 26, 94, 102, 121, 130, 131, 132
universities, 60
urban, 3, 7, 9, 12, 86, 87
urban areas, 86, 87

V

vacancies, 99
valuation, 124
value added tax, 138
VAT, 118
vehicles, 12, 138
ventilation, 39
vessels, 6, 86, 137
victims, ix, 14, 24, 34, 36, 46, 47, 60, 71, 74, 75, 79, 98
videos, 53
videotape, 74
Vietnam, 5, 6, 16, 17, 25, 28, 30, 39, 62, 113
violence, vii, viii, ix, 1, 2, 3, 8, 9, 12, 13, 14, 15, 28, 33, 34, 36, 43, 45, 49, 51, 68, 71, 72, 93, 98, 100, 101, 102, 128, 134
Volunteers, 50

vote, 8, 64, 65
voters, 13, 65, 79
vulnerability, 86, 89

W

wages, 72, 82, 83, 84, 85, 87, 88, 135, 136
waiver, 108
war, 17, 23, 35, 77, 84
warlords, 27
Washington, viii, 2, 5, 31
waste, 121
water, x, 39, 61, 68, 105
water purification, 39
weakness, 69
wealth, 67, 127
weapons, 6, 17, 19, 25, 49, 101
web, 28, 117
websites, 8
welfare, 59, 78, 84, 86, 87, 137
Western countries, 122
wholesale, 88, 138
withdrawal, 18, 25, 113
witnesses, 46, 47, 74
work environment, 85
worker rights, ix, 34
workers, ix, 26, 34, 41, 44, 58, 60, 63, 68, 72, 73, 77, 80, 81, 82, 83, 84, 85, 86, 87, 88, 89, 90, 110, 121, 135, 136, 137
workforce, 84
working conditions, 83, 86, 90
working hours, 137
workplace, 89, 137
World Bank, 112, 133, 135, 136
World War I, 6
worldwide, 132, 135
wrongdoing, 47
WTO, 116, 122

Y

young people, 103

Z

Zone 1, 119
Zone 2, 119
Zone 3, 119